The Anatomy of a Riot

The Anatomy of a Riot:

A Detroit Judge's Report

By JAMES H. LINCOLN

McGraw-Hill Book Company
New York   Toronto   London   Sydney

KFM
4799
.W32
C75

THE ANATOMY OF A RIOT

Copyright © 1968 by James H. Lincoln
All Rights Reserved. Printed in the United States of America.
No part of this publication may be reproduced, stored in a
retrieval system, or transmitted, in any form or by any means,
electronic, mechanical, photocopying, recording or otherwise,
without the prior written permission of the publisher.

Library of Congress Catalog Card Number: 68-9436
First Edition   37885

57254

To those concerned

Preface

Two weeks after the Detroit Riot ended, a Juvenile Court judge from another state came to Detroit because he needed some of the information contained in this report. He could not wait for publication because an advocate of violence was scheduled to talk in his city, where there had already been disturbances.

Present urban conditions have compelled many Juvenile Court judges in the nation to develop comprehensive procedures for handling juveniles brought to their Courts or Youth Homes during a riot. In Michigan the Juvenile Court judge is in charge of the Youth Home in his county. In some other states the Juvenile Court judge must make plans and organize procedures with those who have the responsibility for operating the Youth Home.

Each Court and Youth Home must tailor its procedures and operations to its resources and particular problems. I had a written riot procedure a year before the riot and had conferred with city and county law-enforcement agencies. The fact that there had been some preplanning was invaluable when the crisis came. Even so, we had not foreseen many problems that developed, and many of our procedures were faulty. At the end of the riot, the Youth Home and Court were operating with far greater efficiency than at the beginning of the disturbance. This report contains information and recommendations that will enable Juvenile Court judges everywhere to better prepare for the possibility that their staffs and facilities may one day be confronted with hundreds of juveniles, with little or no advance warning.

Although many portions of this report are addressed primarily to Juvenile Court judges, all of it is addressed *To those concerned.*

The figures concerning the numbers arrested in various categories differ in this report. The Wayne County Prosecutor uses total arrests for all of the 43 communities in Wayne County. The Detroit police report uses only those arrests made in Detroit. The Youth Home statistics do not include juveniles arrested by the police and released at the precinct station. Nor do the Youth Home statistics reflect juveniles brought to the Youth Home by police but not admitted. Whenever statistics are used, the source is identified. The figures differ because they measure different groupings of rioters.

I gratefully acknowledge the assistance of Kim Lincoln, Bernard G. Conley, Joseph Findling, Fay Foster, Norman Krandall, Jean Pacifico, Samuel L. Simpson, and David P. Stoller. Dr. Richard Komisaruk, Arjay Miller, and William L. Cahalan have furnished invaluable reference material. I am grateful to the many employees of the Juvenile Court and the Youth Home for their outstanding work during the 1967 Detroit Riot.

Contents

Part Four: Appendix   107

Part One: Introduction

View from the roof of
the Youth Home—sixth floor

Nighttime Detroit presented a weird scene during the riot. The fires and smoke were most intense along Twelfth Street and Linwood. Other heavy concentrations of fire existed on the east side of Detroit; fires were spotted everywhere. There were intermittent sounds of gunfire. The streets in the area of the Juvenile Court were largely deserted and through the windows of houses shone no light, even shortly after sundown. Figures passed carrying loot; one was blowing a horn. From time to time police cars and ambulances, sirens wailing, passed down the Chrysler Expressway or along surface streets. Firetrucks and firefighting equipment often moved down the side streets without either lights or sirens operating. This was done in the hope of avoiding the sniper fire that was often directed at firefighters during the riot. Within the Youth Home, the gymnasiums and auditoriums were filled with juveniles sleeping on the floor without mattresses and in their own clothing. United States paratroopers and National Guardsmen were stationed both within and without the Youth Home, having observation posts on the roof and throughout a two-block area.

At night the view from the sixth floor of the Youth Home gave one the sensation of being under siege.

Why the riot?

There are at least 500 causes of crime, delinquency, and riots.

It would make more sense to ask *"Why did the forces which had for so long preserved the peace fail to do so in Detroit in July 1967?"*

There is a variety of opinions, but a number of points are clear:

1. Professional agitators did not start the riot.

2. A few professional agitators moved in and took advantage of a riot situation and played a very considerable part in enlarging the riot in the original riot area. They also played a part in spreading it throughout other areas of Detroit.

3. One of the tactics successfully used by professional agitators was to get store windows broken in as many areas of the city as possible. People were attracted like flies to honey by broken store windows and the opportunity to loot.

4. The riot started when the police raided a blind pig in the early morning hours on Twelfth Street, a high-crime-rate poverty area. At one point the situation appeared under control. There are several versions of why it started

up again. The fact that a store was set on fire appears to be a very considerable factor. Bricks and bottles were thrown at firemen. Police moved in to protect firemen. More fires started. The mob grew. Fires started on Grand River and elsewhere. Fires draw crowds and increase excitement. *Fires and broken store windows were decisive factors in enlarging and spreading the riot.*

5. In 1966, approximately a year before the 1967 riot, there had been a riot situation on Kercheval Street on the east side of Detroit. The tactic in 1966 was to use a minimal amount of police. Negro leaders entered the area and calmed the situation. In 1967, on Twelfth Street, appeals from Negro leaders that the people go home had no effect whatsoever. The initial disturbance was far greater in 1967. It should have been apparent fairly early that Twelfth Street was no Kercheval.

6. *WHAT PART DID POVERTY PLAY IN THE RIOT?* The homes in the rear of the Twelfth Street businesses are substantially constructed and in reasonably good repair. They are better constructed than the home in which I lived for more than half my life. The greater portion of adults and juveniles arrested during the riot had jobs and many of them had good jobs. The vast majority of juveniles brought to the Youth Home during the riot did not have a juvenile record and most of them had at least one parent gainfully employed. Most of them were admitted to the Youth Home with money in their pockets that they themselves had earned. These facts would tend to show that poverty was not one of the controlling factors in the riot, but let us look beneath the surface and examine what lies there.

Crime, delinquency, and riots are similar to a mulligan stew in that many factors are mixed up together, and, once mixed, can never be completely sorted out. Twelfth Street itself had all the appearances and elements of a poverty street even if the homes in the rear of the street did not. Records reveal that less than sixty out of 700 juveniles brought to the Court during the riot were on probation. I have no proof but it is an educated guess that hits close to the center of the target that a smaller percentage of the people arrested were criminals and case-hardened delinquents than citizens who had no police record and who were less skilled in avoiding arrest. Furthermore, few arrests were made until the riot had been in progress for many hours, and after middle-class and normally law-abiding citizens had become heavily involved in looting. The police did not start bringing juveniles to the Youth Home until nearly 7:00 P.M. and the riot had been boiling since the early hours of the morning. No one can give an accurate description of the rioter who was not arrested and this includes almost all of those who started it.

It is impossible to obtain eyewitness observers or historians who agree on the part that various factors have played in any great upheaval. Some historians will play down the part that slavery played in bringing on the Civil War, and other historians will assert that slavery was the controlling factor. If historians can't agree on the causes of this upheaval after a century of intensive study, then it is certain that there will never be agreement on the causes of riots or crime and delinquency. There will be endless discussion concerning the part that poverty, school dropouts, militants, middle-class citizens, etc., etc., played.

It is now the subject of congressional hearings and will be the subject of doctoral theses and historians for many years to come.

At this point in time, we are unable to apply the scientific approach to the study of human behavior in the same manner or with the same degree of certainty that it is applied to chemical reactions. For one thing, there are no completely impartial observers. Unfortunately, the mere amassing of a multitude of data (the almanac approach) does not necessarily lead to understanding.

However, it is unnecessary to make exacting evaluations of the multitude of factors that work together to produce a riot. It is sufficient for practical purposes to identify the major factors with some degree of certainty. This can be done. Poverty certainly played a major role in the riot.

The subject of poverty will be discussed more fully in another portion of this report. It will be sufficient for the present to point out that it is as absurd to assert that poverty played no part in the riot as it would be to assert that the slavery issue played no part in bringing about the Civil War. It is asinine to try to measure the part that poverty played solely by a statistical analysis of the income of those arrested. It's like saying that throwing a barrel of gasoline on tons of combustible material had nothing to do with the conflagration. The gasoline is not only combustible itself but it makes all the material it touches combustible. The fact that the percentage of Negroes living in poverty is four times as great as the percentage of whites living in poverty makes the entire Negro community more combustible. There is not as yet full acceptance of middle-class and professional Negroes by many whites. This condition is in no small part based on the image of the Negro living in crime and poverty in the slums. As long as the percentage of Negroes living in poverty is four times as great as the percentage of whites living in poverty, there will exist the necessary ingredients for riots in the entire Negro population—anger, hostility, and rebellion that have their roots in nonacceptance.

"The poor ye have with you always"—but they are not invited. Nonacceptance and poverty are Siamese twins. Poverty is the propagator of rebellion and hostility. Poverty was a major factor in the 1967 Detroit Riot and will continue to be a major factor in civic disorders.

7. No action was taken by the police at the beginning to stop the looting of stores. Tear gas was not used, nor was there any shooting. As soon as it became apparent that *looting was permissible,* normally law-abiding citizens started to loot. Crowds quickly appeared in every area of the city where store windows had been broken. Normally law-abiding citizens thus played a major role in the riot. The number of looters made the mob unmanageable.

8. Once a riot is triggered and there is a breakdown of law and order—anarchy—middle-class citizens, including many homeowners in middle-class neighborhoods, will get involved in looting—at least if looting is permissible in the sense that no arrests will be made if there is a crowd.

9. The snipers did not kill many people considering the amount of shooting done. Some may have been shooting without aiming to create a disturbance. Some may never

before have fired a rifle and were poor shots. Some meant business. On July 26, 1967 at approximately 3:57 P.M., two National Guardsmen were hit by a sniper while standing in front of the Tenth Precinct. At the same time, a policeman was hit several blocks away. The circumstances were such that it is probable that the same sniper hit all three of them.

10. It has been asserted that the burning of stores was directed at stores that had sharp credit practices and were price-gougers. This was not true in most cases. I have shopped in some of those burned stores for many years, and some of them offered as good a bargain, on as favorable terms, as one could get anywhere in Detroit.

Obviously, some stores may have been burned because of hostility to the owners or their business practices. There may well have been mixed motives. Every arsonist in the city had a chance to have a field day, and undoubtedly some fires were set by them with no motive other than to watch the fire. Some disturbed individuals undoubtedly did some shooting with little or no motive whatsoever. People act from several motives quite as often as they act from a single motive. Anyone who tries to arrange motives for the rioters in a neat pattern or package does not give an accurate account. The course the riot took and the motives of the rioters are highly complex subjects. The inability to give a clear answer to these questions is one of the reasons we ask: "Why did the forces which had for so long preserved the peace fail to do so in Detroit in July 1967?" instead of "Why the riot?"

11. The main thrust of the riot was against stores, police, firemen, and the military. Thus the riot took on the

aspects of a directed rebellion, but in fact little direction was given by anyone. The ideas and pronouncement of professional agitators over the preceding year or so were undoubtedly a factor in increasing the unrest, but the actual course of the riot was not to any great degree determined by leadership.

12. The percentage of whites in the riot was small. The Detroit police arrested 40 male white juveniles and 582 male Negro juveniles. They arrested 550 male white adults and 4683 male Negro adults. As a group the white community thought the thrust of the riot was against white citizens. They stayed home. However, the whites who did become involved were not attacked by the Negroes. They looted together in the best of camaraderie. In one police precinct the white and Negro snipers had one of the best relationships. The vast majority of both the Negro and white community stayed out of the riot. However, Detroit is the fifth largest city in the nation, and a small percentage of either Negroes or whites in Detroit adds up to tens of thousands of people. There were 703 juveniles and 5967 adults arrested by the Detroit police.

One thing is clear. It was definitely an adult riot, if one uses age seventeen as the dividing line between juveniles and adults. In Michigan, those under seventeen, are handled by Juvenile Courts, and those seventeen and over are handled in adult courts. Delinquency is only a mirror of the adult population. One look at the riot and it is easier to answer "Why delinquency?" than "Why the riot?"

It is futile to attempt to draw a portrait of a rioter. There are dozens, if not hundreds, of variables.

13. The division between Negro extremists (snipers, arsonists, and the like) and middle-class Negroes is as wide as their differences with middle-class white citizens. In one police precinct in Detroit, hundreds of prisoners were locked up for several days. The white and colored snipers grouped together in friendly fashion. The Negro snipers talked about getting some "Negro fat cats" when they got out. Their hatred against middle-class Negroes was very deep, but they accepted white snipers as friends. This was not very comforting to middle-class Negroes locked up in the same precinct for curfew violations; this happened to some law-abiding citizens during the riot. On one hand they face a white backlash; and on the other they face extremists in their own race who would like to burn them out or otherwise harm them.

14. *The atmosphere in Detroit was more conducive to a riot in 1967 than in 1966.*

   A. To an ever-increasing degree the spokesmen for the poverty areas, both Negro and white, practiced and advocated lawbreaking as a means to gain their ends. This group included members of the clergy.

   B. Some Negro leaders openly advocated violence and were given far more attention in the news media than Negro leaders who would prefer to obtain their objectives by lawful means.

   C. A very considerable segment of the extreme leadership preached a doctrine of "hate whitey," and also advocated setting up an "antistructure" within the nation. In other words, the objective would not be to bring Negroes into the mainstream of American life but rather would exclude all white influence in the Negro community, including schoolteachers, police, and the like. In other words, without explaining how it could be achieved, Negroes were to be entirely separated from the white community and yet somehow have all the benefits of being in the mainstream of American life—which sounds very much like the situation that exists in South Africa (*apartheid*) except that in some unexplained way, the Negroes would have all the benefits of being in the mainstream of American life. The Negro leaders who advocate this course of action are correct in their assumption that violence would be necessary to move in that direction. The goal is obviously unattainable in that an "antistructure" within a civilization must join in the general objectives of the civilization or be left behind. The answer of black nationalist advocates to this is that a large percentage of the Negroes are behind now, a point that carries great weight in poverty areas. The issue then resolves itself as to whether Negroes believe they can gain their way into the mainstream, or if their best hope lies in setting up an "antistructure." (It is impossible to describe this proposed antistructure because its advocates do not spell it out. But it is very clear that the process of getting it involves violence, lawbreaking, and a doctrine of "hate whitey.")

The area of discontent is far wider than the poverty area, but the poverty area is where the heat is on and where the real struggle for leadership and direction will be decided.

In July 1967, total discontent in the poverty areas in Detroit was greater than in 1966, and the response by the people to a riot situation was more difficult to handle.

Thus, for a number of reasons, the forces that had kept peace in Detroit and avoided a riot since 1943 failed to function effectively in July 1967.

The flow of events during the riot

It began with a call from the Youth Bureau of the Police Department to the Judge's home at 1:15 P.M. on a warm Sunday in July. The tempo of events increased as personnel in the Youth Home and Court were notified. By 5 P.M. there was acceptance of the fact that there was a city-wide riot and it would be necessary for the Judge and some of the supervisors to proceed to the Court and Youth Home with the knowledge that they would not be returning home for a few days, perhaps a week.

The trip across the city to the Youth Home in a squad car gave the Judge a better estimate of the situation than twenty phone conversations with the police. He saw two looters breaking into a store and mentioned it to the policemen with whom he was riding. One replied that they could not shoot. There were in fact no such instructions to the police, but some police thought that they would be in serious difficulty if they were to shoot looting rioters who resisted arrest.

This was the first time I ever saw a felony being committed with police on hand without the police acting. At this time I also learned that tear gas was not being used.

Thus, even before viewing the main riot area one became aware that the breakdown of law and order was complete.

Within several blocks, the smoke could be seen rolling in heavy clouds from Twelfth Street toward Woodward Avenue. The magnitude of the disturbance was now brought home with the impact of a bomb. The police radio brought news of the riot spreading to points all over the city.

Once at the Youth Home, all was quiet. It was to be hours before juveniles would be arrested in any number and conveyed to the Youth Home. There was some time for thought and preparation.

When the juveniles came, they came in great numbers. A riot is a changing thing. The tempo of activity and the need to make decisions and constant re-evaluations increased throughout the crisis. It took direct, clear orders to get employees to change from normal procedures that were inadequate in a riot. There was the gradual recognition that the staff was responding to the crisis and that the usual complaints were forgotten because of the singleness of purpose of all to do what was necessary to meet the crisis.

There was frustration caused by the breakdown of communications—twenty phone calls would produce nineteen busy signals due to overload of circuits. The anxiety of knowing that a very dangerous situation existed in the Youth Home was heightened by the lack of security personnel and the inability to reach the Governor, the Mayor, the Police Commissioner, etc., electronically, with requests for manpower aid. There were problems of getting employees to work, particularly after curfew hours; food problems; problems of handling the questions of hundreds of parents looking for their children. There were judicial decisions to be made and instructions to be given to Referees. Then, as the riot drew to a close, the work of the Court and Youth Home began. There was a need for an immediate review of the cases of all juveniles in the Youth Home; this continued for several days after the streets of the city were again still.

Through the riot, there had been constant re-evaluation, not only of the situation in the Court and Youth Home, but of the general situation in the community and the effect conditions in each would have upon the other. Would the disturbance result in some assault on the Youth Home or a sniper firing into one of the windows? Would it be necessary to transport some juveniles to another location either during or soon after the riot? The knowledge that the juveniles were playing no part in the shooting and virtually none in the burning came only after the riot had passed its peak.

Only after the riot did it become clear that the juveniles were, for the most part, looters and curfew violators. Most of them had never been in Court before and probably never will be again. They were caught up in the riot and looted because adults were looting, and if they were in a crowd, no one stopped them. Some looted with their parents or other relatives. Nearly all were arrested within walking distance of their homes.

In the riot procedure I had outlined on July 29, 1966, a year before the riot, this statement of policy was made and adhered to rigidly during the riot:

Whenever a juvenile may be legally held and his release would tend to promote further civic disorder, it will be the policy to detain him in the Youth Home regardless of the extraordinary means that must be taken to provide space and facilities.

The policy statement also states:

Juveniles still retain constitutional and legal rights during civic disorders. There will be Preliminary Hearings the day following admittance to see if each juvenile should be held until his regular hearing.

These basic decisions were adhered to during the riot, even though the Youth Home population for boys reached 681 in a space designed for 160.

No one was released who could *legally and properly* be held, and the judicial process continued during the riot with full recognition that constitutional and legal rights were not suspended by the riot. The riot began on Sunday, July 23, 1967, and the tempo of activity at the Court and Youth Home continued at the same level until several days after the riot ended. By Monday, July 31, 1967, a week after the riot began, everything was as normal at the Court and Youth Home as in any military operation after a major battle.

Part Two:
Judicial and Custodial Handling of Juveniles during Riot

Police procedures relative to juveniles during the riot

1. Michigan law requires that the police convey juveniles under the age of seventeen to the Juvenile Court or the Youth Home "forthwith." The Juvenile Court judge is responsible for the operation of the Youth Home and the Court.

2. During the riot, juveniles were taken by the arresting officers to the police precinct stations and turned over to the Police Youth Bureau officers. The only purpose for taking juveniles to the police stations was to process the necessary papers to get them admitted to the Youth Home. They were not locked up with adult prisoners. Police took no statements from juveniles after arrest that they attempted to put in evidence in Court. They processed the juveniles as rapidly as possible and the Court received no complaints concerning the treatment of juveniles while at the police stations or while being conveyed from the stations to the Youth Home.

The only complaints by juveniles concerning police referred to time of arrest.

3. Dr. Perry P. Burnstine was responsible for giving medical care to all boys brought to the Youth Home dur-

ing the riot who were injured or for any reason requested medical attention. There were some cut by glass while going through broken store windows to loot. Dr. Burnstine and the nursing staff at the Youth Home reported "less than thirteen" cases where juveniles complained of rough treatment by police. None of these juveniles had serious injuries.

The three referees who heard some 700 Preliminary Hearings during the riot confirm the report of Dr. Burnstine. They report "less than fifteen" complaints by juveniles of rough police treatment.

One boy who complained of rough treatment by the police admitted that he was resisting arrest with a six-inch dagger. When juveniles resist arrest, police must use force necessary to effect the arrests and complaints are likely to result.

One boy was taken directly to the City Hospital and then brought to the Youth Home three days later. He had been badly beaten by either the police or the National Guard. A thorough investigation disclosed nothing further because of the boy's inability to identify anyone. This was a clear-cut case of severe abuse. A thorough investigation produced no evidence of a law violation by the boy. There was no case comparable to this in the 700 cases brought to Juvenile Court. The case stands out as exceptional to the usual treatment given juveniles during the riot.

4. It is very clear that there was no general abuse of juveniles by police or National Guard during the riot. This statement is still true, even though there may have been

some cases of abuse that did not come to the Court's attention.

5. Every attempt has been made to confine this report to matters on which I am able to speak with authority and therefore does not include any report of treatment of adults arrested and held at precinct stations during the riot. The law in Michigan requiring that juveniles be brought to the Youth Home "forthwith" is rigidly enforced by the Wayne County Juvenile Court. Thus, under Michigan law, both juveniles and police have considerable protection—there is far less chance of abuse of juveniles than adults, and there is far less chance of police having to face false charges of abuse of juveniles than there is by adults. Many adults were locked up in precinct stations for days during the riot. Juveniles were in stations a few hours at the most. While at the stations, they were in the hands of Youth Bureau officers and I have not had a complaint against a Youth Bureau officer in five years.

6. There was much hostility directed at the police by the juveniles arrested during the riot. The Clinic for Child Study of the Wayne County Juvenile Court did a study of the attitudes of the juveniles arrested during the riot. Dr. Richard Komisaruk, director of the Clinic, reported very strong hostility directed at the police. The juveniles often felt the police were brutal. However, not a single case of alleged abuse was referred by the Clinic to the Court. Dr. Komisaruk's report is accurate from what I have observed. Dr. Komisaruk is reporting the attitudes of the juveniles and not what actually happened. No one blesses a policeman for even a traffic ticket and certainly no one

is going to bless a policeman who gets him locked up. However, the feeling against the police is so intense that there are obviously many factors involved. The police are symbols of the white-power structure that was under attack in the riot.

The attitudes of the juveniles mirrored the attitudes of their parents and adults involved in the riot.

There was much talk of police abuse during the riot. Many parents, prior to the Preliminary Hearings, and before they had the opportunity to talk with their sons, were convinced that their sons had been abused. Since the riot, I have spoken in a number of neighborhoods where many juveniles were arrested during the riot. There was apparent and open hostility expressed against the police.

Police-community relations have become one of the most important and most difficult problems in the nation. This point clearly emerged in the 1967 riot.

7. After delivering the boys to the Intake of the Youth Home, the police returned to their precincts for further riot duty, and the juveniles became the responsibility of Juvenile Court.

Problems of Youth Home, Intake and Release, during the riot

The following orders should be given immediately before a backup starts at Intake:

1. *Eliminate showers for juveniles at Intake.*
2. *Eliminate medical examinations except for the injured.*
3. *Eliminate changes of clothing. Admit juveniles to Youth Home in their own clothing.*
4. *Give orders not to move juveniles about in Youth Home after assignment to a particular location.*

The following steps should be taken immediately to forestall later administrative problems:

1. *Short cut all paper work! Conduct the entire operation—Intake, Release, and judicial from one basic document—the police admittance sheet.*
2. *Xerox seven copies or more of the police admittance sheet as soon as a juvenile is admitted.*
   A. Be certain that location of the juvenile in Youth Home is written on original before it is Xeroxed.
   B. Number copies.
3. *See that copies of the police admittance sheet are distributed immediately and kept in alphabetical order.*

A. *The Judge*: one copy.

B. *The Referee* in the hearing room in Youth Home: two copies.

C. *Intake*: one copy.

D. *Release Desk*: one copy.

E. *The typist* making up permanent record cards for Youth Home: one copy.

F. *The Case Work Services Unit*: one copy. Keep all copies in alphabetical order at all times.

4. Have Hearing Officers write disposition in longhand on two copies of police admittance sheet at Preliminary Hearing and give one copy to Release Desk. Thus, Release Desk will have admittance sheets on all juveniles admitted to Youth Home and a *second* pile of admission sheets on juveniles who have had Preliminary Hearings.

Hundreds of parents will be coming to the Release Desk. Some will falsely state that they have not been to a Preliminary Hearing and the workers at the Release Desk can quickly check the stack of admission sheets furnished by the Referees and find the facts noted on them.

Of course, there will be another complete and separate record of admission sheets on everyone admitted to the Youth Home, with the location of the juvenile therein noted upon it.

Personnel and space problems of Intake and Release Desk:

1. Intake and Release should be on opposite sides of the Youth Home. This eliminates the congestion.

2. The usual space allocations are insufficient. There may be a backup of 75 boys in an Intake area made to handle 20; there may be 200 parents at the Release Desk.

    A. Put benches outside building for parents at Release side of the building.

    B. If possible, transfer typing of permanent record cards from Intake to another office. Handle elsewhere as much record-keeping on property of juveniles as possible.

3. Assign additional personnel (Probation Officers, typists, etc.) to Intake and Release Desk soon after a riot begins.

Recognize the fact that the work at the Release Desk is going to increase as the riot draws to a close

Hold a staff meeting of supervisors at 9 A.M. each day. There will be need for constant re-evaluation of the situation and shifts in personnel. If Probation Officers are used in the Youth Home at Intake and Release, there will be no need for volunteer help.

A Xerox machine with 10,000 sheets of duplicating material and an operator are needed in or near Intake.

The efficiency with which paper work and Intake and Release are handled will in large measure determine the quality of justice during a riot. You cannot explain to a juvenile that he was not given a hearing for thirty hours because he could not be located or because of an error in paper work.

Keep the record, the juvenile, and the Hearing Officer in the same building. Do not get involved in the delays and problems caused by transporting juveniles for their judicial hearings from one building to another during a riot. *Take the Judge or the Hearing Officer to the prisoner and not the prisoner to the Judge in time of riot.*

Look for the procedures that will cut through red tape and paper work.

Operation of Youth Home during the riot

Space needs in the Youth Home

The sudden heavy influx of youth causes an acute need of floor space. The following things should be done in the order enumerated:

1. Double or triple the occupancy of the wards. (During the 1967 riot, wards with a capacity of 18 accommodated as many as 50 boys.)

2. Once the wards are filled, use gymnasiums and auditoriums in the Youth Home. (Hundreds of boys slept on the floor of the gymnasiums and auditoriums.)

3. When and if gymnasiums and auditoriums are utilized, the enclosed playgrounds may be turned into confinement areas. Inclement weather presents no problems, for riots do not occur, as a practical matter, during such weather. (It was not necessary to use the playgrounds in the 1967 riot except as a place to provide exercise for the boys.)

Internal security

The regular staff is tried tremendously during an emergency such as the riot of 1967. Its numbers, even when applied in double shifts, are inadequate. A substantial amount of outside help will be required to insure the satisfactory operation of the Youth Home.

Recommendation: It is recommended that there be a definite arrangement or pattern of riot procedure among the Court, the Sheriff, and the National Guard. Admittedly, the participation of the Guard depends upon the Governor's mandate. Once that is given, however, the responsibility of the Guard would be to bring about the quick execution of the prearranged plan. The police and Sheriff are going to be busy with the adults in a riot: only a minimum amount of help can be expected from them. *This means that the chief source of additional manpower must come from the National Guard.* It is most helpful to have available even a small number of Deputy Sheriffs who know the Youth Home. The National Guard will need to be assigned to work with the Youth Home attendants and the Deputy Sheriffs. It is strongly recommended that there be sufficient National Guardsmen and other manpower in every ward, gymnasium, Intake, etc., so that no one will attempt any disturbance whatsoever.

External security of Youth Home and Court during riot

During the 1967 riot, several anonymous phone calls were made to the Court demanding that all juveniles be released; the term "black power" was mentioned. There was little chance of an assault being made on the Youth Home or Court with the thought of anyone forcing his way into the building, but firebombs or sniping presented a distinct possibility.

The problem of external security was handled by 32 paratroopers; later they were replaced by National Guardsmen. They posted men throughout the two-block area of the Youth Home and Court. A number of observations should be made concerning external security:

1. There is no possible way to stop a sniper from shooting holes in the windows of a six-story Youth Home several hundred yards away. However, a well-armed force around the building—men with jeeps, telephone communications to a central command post, loaded rifles, etc. —would be a deterrent to snipers operating in the area. It should also be able to protect the area from firebombs quite easily.

2. The paratroopers assigned to Juvenile Court during the 1967 riot were well equipped and had been battle-trained in Vietnam. They were the best the nation had to offer.

3. The National Guardsmen who later replaced the paratroopers were poorly equipped. They were short of transportation. They had no telephone equipment. They were under orders to keep their rifles unloaded and had to check with their Commanding Officer, possibly two blocks away, before taking any counteraction. They were paper dolls so far as furnishing external security was concerned, except that snipers did not know the orders and handicaps under which they operated. Thus their presence did serve a purpose.

There has been much criticism of the National Guard in the Detroit newspapers since the riot. The National

Guard assigned to Juvenile Court, both for internal and external security during the riot, did an excellent job. They went about their assignments in a very businesslike manner. They worked long hours without complaint and slept on the floor of one of the auditoriums in the Youth Home when they were fortunate enough to be relieved. They did an excellent job; they merit less criticism and more support. Specifically, they should be supplied with the equipment necessary to do their job. It is nonsense to put a Guardsman on a post without telephone communication, with an unloaded rifle, and then put him under orders to do nothing even if a sniper begins firing on the building except to walk two blocks and get instructions from his Commanding Officer.

Salvation Army. Three National Guardsmen who had been in the Twelfth Street area had strong praise for the work of the Salvation Army. Two of them said they were going to give the Salvation Army a special donation when they returned home. The Salvation Army fed everyone it could, without question, during the riot.

The Court Chaplains also merit special note. They put in long, hard hours and performed any task requested of them.

Bedding and sanitation problems

1. Most of the boys will be sleeping on the floor without mattresses. No harmful effects came from this in the 1967 riot.

2. The sanitary facilities serve a dual purpose: they clean the guests and also keep them occupied. Keep ro-

tating the boys through showers during the day and evening. It occupies their time and they like it. There are showers in rooms adjoining the gymnasiums in the Youth Home. It took a full day to get all the boys through the showers. Showers were eliminated at Intake during the riot; there was no time for showers at the time the boys were admitted. The showers were given only after they had been admitted to the Youth Home.

Medical problems in the Youth Home

1. The hospitals will be overloaded and only the very severely injured can be taken to a hospital.

2. A large number of juveniles will be cut by glass from climbing in and out of store windows. Many others will develop headaches, stomach aches, etc.

3. Keep one doctor on duty in the daytime; nurses must be on duty around the clock in the Clinic of the Youth Home. There will be several hundred juveniles who will need attention.

Problems of occupying the time of boys locked in Youth Home during a riot

1. Have them take showers.

2. It will take a considerable length of time to give them food three times a day.

3. They should be given a Preliminary Hearing within 24 hours of the time they are admitted to the Youth Home.

4. The Court Chaplains are very helpful. Clinic personnel, counselors, etc., should be used as much as possible.

57254

5. Have television sets operating through the day and evening in all wards, gymnasiums, etc., where there are juveniles.

6. Let the boys walk around the playground for a time during the day. The playgrounds serving the Wayne County Youth Home have high walls and there were plenty of National Guardsmen around. There was no trouble and the practice helped pass the time.

Food problems in Youth Home during a riot

The cooking facilities at the Wayne County Youth Home were designed to accommodate 220 persons per meal. During the riot as many as 900 were served in a single meal (681 boys, more than 100 girls, staff, and National Guardsmen). *The following points must be considered:*

1. Restaurants are closed during a riot.

2. Staff members may be working around the clock and must be fed along with the increased juvenile population.

3. The National Guard had not been fed all day when they arrived at the Youth Home and it was necessary to feed them for several days.

4. Normal food supplies may be shut down. It was necessary for the National Guard to take trucks across Detroit to the Wayne County General Hospital, which helped out by furnishing bread and milk.

5. Everyone—juveniles, staff, and National Guardsmen —got three good warm meals a day while they were at the Youth Home. The galley staff did an excellent job.

6. The Youth Home Director should ascertain, before the influx of population begins, the needs of the cook and meet those needs promptly.

Girls' unit in Youth Home during riot

The ratio of women to men arrested by Detroit Police during the riot was about the same as that for girl juveniles to boy juveniles.

Women arrested   734   Men arrested   5233
Girls arrested   81   Boys arrested   622

These figures only include Detroit arrests, but they accurately reflect the ratio of arrests by sex from July 23 through July 31, 1967, inclusive.

The girls' population in the Youth Home actually dropped during the riot. The police would undoubtedly have picked up more as truants and streetwalkers if there had been no riot.

It may be that a higher proportion of females took part in the riot than is indicated by the arrest figures. The police may have been more reluctant to arrest a kicking, biting female during the riot than to arrest a male who resisted, although this is a conjecture.

The police conveyed fewer than 50 per cent of the girls arrested to the Youth Home during the riot.

Miscellaneous problems concerning Youth-Home management during a riot

1. Lines of communication break down. Youth Home and Court workers will be trying to call the Court and Youth Home from their homes and they will not be able to get through. It will be very difficult to get through to the Governor, the Mayor, the Sheriff, the Police Commissioner, etc., even when there is a very urgent need for additional manpower at the Youth Home. Everyone be-

comes occupied with a multitude of problems that need immediate attention.

2. Problems that are normally minor, such as removing ten boys from the Youth Home to the jail because they threatened an outbreak, may be more difficult to handle during a riot.

3. Youth Home and Court personnel may be stopped by police and National Guardsmen from getting to the Youth Home from their own homes, etc. The Governor will declare a curfew.

Recommendations:

1. Install special phone line direct to Sheriff's Office and Police Commissioner.

2. Install a phone in the Youth Home with an *unlisted number*. Give the employees this number and man the phone shortly after the riot begins. Thus this phone will be clear of the hundreds of calls that will be coming in from people trying to locate their children. This line should not run through the switchboard, but should be an outside line.

3. Have a clear understanding with the Sheriff and National Guard before the riot starts. They must understand that the Youth Home is a critical point and will need additional help shortly after a riot starts.

4. Xerox several hundred letters of identification for Youth Home and Court employees. These letters should have the Judge's signature on them. It will help employees to get about when a curfew is imposed.

5. Hold a staff conference at nine o'clock each morn-

ing during the riot. Include Supervisor of Intake and Release, Youth Home Supervisor, and Court Supervisors together with Referees. The detention functions, the Release and Intake functions, and judicial functions will all be going on in the same building. There will be a considerable amount of complaining about what others are doing or not doing, and many of these matters can be worked out by a conference.

6. There will be announcements on television and radio telling everyone to stay home during the riot. *Issue specific instructions to both Youth Home and Court employees to come to work regardless of announcements on television and radio.*

Of course, many will not show up and it will be necessary to work Youth Home attendants double shifts. Probation Officers can be used at Intake and Release Desks. There may be 100 parents to talk to at one time. Keep anyone who shows up; any sent home will probably be needed a short time later. Keep a number of secretaries, typists, Xerox operators, etc., on hand. They will be needed.

Judicial problems during the riot

Besides being responsible for the Youth Home and the operation of Intake and Release, a Juvenile Court Judge is also responsible for safeguarding the constitutional and legal rights of juveniles brought to the Youth Home during a riot. The quality of justice administered by a Juvenile Court during a riot depends on proper administration as well as proper judicial decisions. It is impossible to explain to a juvenile the distinction between legal and administrative injustice. Injustice caused by undue delays in getting a juvenile before a Hearing Officer cannot be tolerated. The purpose of this portion of the report is to lay down guidelines concerning the handling of judicial problems during a riot and to re-emphasize some of the points made concerning administration given in other portions of this report.

Constitutional and statutory rights of juveniles during a riot

Constitutional and statutory rights of juveniles are not suspended during a riot.

38

The juvenile is entitled to a timely Preliminary
Hearing after being admitted to the Youth Home

1. The only judicial work conducted during the riot
will be Preliminary Hearings. The question of accepting
delinquency petitions and all decisions other than questions of detention of juveniles should be postponed until
after the riot.

2. The sole purpose of the Preliminary Hearing is to
determine whether the arrest of the juvenile was legally
justified, make a determination of whether there are sufficient facts to justify the detention of the juvenile, and if
so, to set the terms of release (amount of bail). Juveniles,
except in very rare cases, are entitled to have bail set
by the Court.

3. Assign Referees to work on a full-time basis. Every
juvenile should be brought before a Referee within
twenty-four hours of admittance to Youth Home.

4. All Preliminary Hearings should be held in the Youth
Home. Under no circumstances should juveniles be taken
outside the Youth Home for Preliminary Hearings. Any
attempt to transport 700 juveniles to Court is not feasible.

5. The document before the Referee will be two
Xeroxed copies of the police admittance sheet. The Referee will write the disposition on each sheet, together with
information concerning who was present at the hearing,
etc. One copy will be retained by the Referee; *the second
copy will be taken to the Release Desk, where copies will
be kept in alphabetical order.*

6. Keep the Hearing Officer, the records, and the juvenile in the same building—the Youth Home.

The following papers will be before the Referee:
A. Two copies of the police admittance sheet.
B. The Intake admittance card showing if the juvenile has ever before been admitted to the Youth Home and similar data. (Most of the juveniles arrested during the Detroit riot had never before been admitted to the Youth Home and the only document before the Referee in the vast majority of cases was the police admittance sheet.)

The continued preliminary-hearing technique must be used in time of riot as the only possible means of properly administering justice

The Court is faced with a legal constitutional dilemma caused by the hectic pace of the riot. However, if handled properly, there need be little or no miscarriage of justice.

1. Unless Preliminary Hearings held during the riot are kept to a very minimum length of time, it will be impossible to get hundreds of juveniles before a Hearing Officer for several days after they have been admitted to the Youth Home. The choice is between a brief hearing or great delay in bringing many juveniles before a Hearing Officer.

By a fast screening of cases by Referees, there will be several hundred out of 700 who can be ordered released to parents on personal recognizance. This does not mean that all those ordered released will be taken from the Youth Home, for the parents may not have been at the Preliminary Hearing, and they may not show up at the Youth Home until after the riot draws to a close. *Some are content to use the Court and Youth Home as baby-sitters during the riot.* But, if a Preliminary Hearing was held and the boy ordered released, the Release Desk was given the record of this hearing. They were able to immediately release the boy when the parents appeared after the riot. The judicial work will start when the riot comes to a close, and it is absolutely necessary to clear up as many Preliminary-Hearing questions as possible while the riot is in progress. Three Referees heard 700 Preliminary Hearings during the 1967 riot, with the understanding that decisions were not necessarily final and would be reviewed as the riot came to an end. A majority of the Preliminary Hearings held during the riot will become continued Hearings.

2. The continued-hearing technique is necessary not only because of limitations of time during a riot, but also for two other distinct reasons:

A. Many juveniles may be legally and constitutionally held during the riot under bail bonds that the parents cannot possibly meet during the riot, for banks are closed and bonding companies are overburdened with problems of adult prisoners. Whether the bond is $1000 or $10,000, parents cannot produce it except in about six cases out of 700. There is a complete breakdown of law and order in the community, and during the riot there should be no release of juveniles who might only feed the riot by returning to their looting. *Once law and order are restored, the Court may reduce many bonds or release many on personal recognizance.* Also, more facts will be available on which to make a decision as the riot draws to a close.

B. The law requires that a parent or guardian be present at Preliminary Hearings. However, if the Court waits for parents to appear, the juvenile will be deprived of his legal rights to a timely hearing. The continued Preliminary Hearing technique is the only sensible solution.

The juvenile need not have his constitutional or legal rights violated by reason of the fact that a parent is not present. No record is made of anything he says. He cannot waive his constitutional rights without his parents, and nothing he says would be admissible in the event a delinquency petition is filed.

Even when parents were present, no attempt was made to obtain records of statements for the purpose of using them against the juvenile at a possible later hearing on a delinquency petition. On the average, it would take ten minutes to get the necessary constitutional waivers from parents and juveniles. Seven hundred waivers would take 7000 minutes and in the meantime hundreds of juveniles would be waiting for hearings; this would not be feasible. Preliminary Hearings may not be used for practical reasons as instruments of getting evidence for a delinquency hearing. Hold the Preliminary Hearing whether the parent is present or not, then continue it for further consideration. Review all cases as the riot comes to a close.

Very important note to Juvenile Court Judges

Instruct Referees to tell parents that the Judge will review their decision as to amount of bail as soon as possible, which means as a practical matter when the riot comes to a close. Remember, in only about one case out of a hundred can the parent meet the bail bond during the riot.

In 1967 it appeared that although probable cause existed in almost all cases and the arrests were legal, nevertheless cases could not be made to sustain convictions of hundreds of juveniles brought to the Youth Home during the riot. For this as well as other reasons, every effort must be made to let the parents and juveniles know that the Court is not condoning quick justice in any case, but is doing its very best to administer justice under the most difficult conditions.

There is no legal or constitutional bar to detaining either juveniles or adults on *"information and belief."* It is not necessary to have testimony showing *"probable cause"* for *short-term detentions*. Testimony showing "probable cause" should be produced as quickly as possible to justify detention, regardless of the charge.

The handling of judicial problems as the riot
comes to a close

At this point the Judge's work is just beginning. The Judge will have been occupied with many administrative problems of operating the Youth Home during the riot, conferring with Referees, etc. I stayed at the Court and Youth Home on a twenty-four-hour-a-day basis during the week of the Detroit riot; so did some members of the staff. Judges should have in their chambers a couch that can be used comfortably as a bed in the event they can find a few hours to sleep. Much of the operation was conducted from the Judge's chambers as the Court is physically connected with the Youth Home. As the riot draws to a close a battle-weary Court will have hundreds of bail-bond decisions that need immediate review; hundreds of parents will be collecting around the Intake Desk asking that some decision be made regarding their sons; attorneys will be demanding that consideration be given immediately to their clients.

1. Once again the Judge must turn to his staff (all highly competent people who can furnish information and give recommendations):

   A. The Register, who is also a Referee.
   B. The Referees.
   C. The Casework Department.
   D. The Intake personnel.
   E. The Assistant Prosecutor, assigned to Juvenile Court on a full-time basis.
   F. The Youth Bureau officers of the Detroit Police Department, who are assigned to Juvenile Court.

2. The main thrust should be on those cases that might properly be released on personal recognizance of the parents and juveniles. The Casework Unit and the Intake Unit will effectively screen cases where there are no previous contacts and where the charge is looting—the great bulk of the cases.

A constant flow of police admittance sheets went to the Release Desk marked "$1000 personal recognizance" as the riot drew to a close. The form used is included as

Appendix VII, page 147. There was never any difficulty in producing these juveniles. They even came to the Court Clinic on a voluntary basis when requested.

3. Assign cases involving attorneys to the Register, who is second in command of the Court. Let the Register review the bond set by the Referee and if the attorney still objects, the Judge may then consider the matter. In most cases the Register's recommendation will be accepted by the attorney.

4. There were about a dozen cases where the juvenile was charged with being in possession of burning material, and one boy was charged with attempting to burn a building. The Assistant Prosecutor, working with the Youth Bureau of the Police Department, was invaluable in determining whether or not there was enough evidence to warrant filing a delinquency petition. A review of those cases resulted in recommendations for release on nearly all of them. As matters developed, there were only two cases where there was substantial evidence of juveniles involved in burning. Thus the cases that involved bail bonds were, for the most part, limited to cases of boys who had been on probation. Some of them had pending petitions filed against them for violation of probation at the time they were apprehended during the riot. This information was furnished by the Casework Department to the Judge.

Summary of recommendations to Judges on handling judicial problems during a riot

1. Hold Preliminary Hearings only to determine the amount of the bail bond; leave decisions on whether or not to accept delinquency petitions until after the riot.

2. Continue all Preliminary Hearings held during the riot where bail bond has been set for review of bond amount. Inform parents that there will be a review of each case by the Judge as quickly as possible, which means as the riot draws to a close, or when the flow of juveniles being brought to the Youth Home diminishes.

3. Hold Preliminary Hearings within twenty-four hours of the time the juvenile is admitted to the Youth Home. Have the Referees hold them every day, all day.

4. Hold all Preliminary Hearings in the Youth Home or detention facility. Keep the Hearing Officer, the records, and the juvenile in the same building. Do not move any juvenile from the Youth Home for the purpose of a hearing.

5. It is not possible to generalize the amount of bail— each case must be decided on its own merits. In any event it is virtually impossible for parents to get a bail bond while the riot is in process.

Recommended administrative procedures supportive of legal procedures

Paper work should be kept at a minimum. The police admittance sheet should be the sole document relating to the juvenile in use during the emergency. Copies should be given to the appropriate positions in the total process. Intake, judicial matters, release, etc., should all be handled from this one basic document. As the riot draws to a close the operation must be so conducted that the Judge has before him, in alphabetical order, a copy of the police admittance sheets with the notations of Referees' decisions on them.

Locate Intake and Release operations on opposite sides of the facility in which the juveniles are housed. These points should be so staffed that there will be little congestion at either operation. This insures maximum internal security and facilitates the judicial objectives stated above.

Juveniles should not be relocated or reassigned in the detention facility once their area has been designated at the Intake Desk and noted on the police admittance sheet. Following any other policy would frustrate efforts to hold timely hearings for all and to achieve an efficient release of any juvenile when his parents or attorney requests it.

Importance of unity of command

There is great advantage in having the entire Juvenile Court operation under the direction of the Juvenile Court Judge, particularly during a riot. Intake, custody, administration of the judicial process, and release are interrelated problems. Unity of command makes it possible to effect decisions promptly and fixes the responsibility for the total operation on one individual.

Part Three:
The ABC of It!

Millions of Americans do not feel personally involved in the crisis that confronts America. The majority are living outside the core areas of cities in which riots occur. Millions view the problem in the same detached manner that they view the problem of placing a man on the moon. There are undoubtedly many factors contributing to the general mood of the nation. Whatever the reasons, it is very apparent that America has little intention of really coming to grips with its problems in the immediate future.

No one can predict when there will be any substantial change in the present mood of the American people, but it is safe to predict that there will be a gradual, substantial, although not dramatic deterioration and worsening of conditions that constitute our present difficulties.

At some point there *will* be a marked shift in the public mood. It may come gradually, or it may come abruptly as it did in 1929 when the Depression broke upon the nation or in 1941 at Pearl Harbor. Perhaps, this time, it will come gradually and not be punctuated by some major disaster.

Maybe nothing as dramatic as a stock market crash or Pearl Harbor will happen, but the crisis is just as dangerous and just as real. Many of us would like to see an America where the chief concern of its citizens is directed to achievement. Today, the chief concern is directed to behavior problems. In 1968, the major issue in the elections may well be crime, delinquency, and riots. If there were no such issues, the major issue might then be which party or candidate would help bring about the greatest educational opportunity for all Americans. Throughout its history, the focus of attention in America has been on achievement of its citizens, not behavior problems. The change in focus of attention in itself constitutes a basic change in American life.

We will now pass through a trying time when there is unlikely to be any really effective action taken to resolve our problems. It will be a time of speeches by candidates who will deplore the decline in respect for public authority and law in America—a sound, vote-catching theme that fits the mood of the day. I am in complete agreement, but it will take something besides speeches to solve our problems.

There is simply no way to insure respect for law and order by government fiat or by making speeches about it. If there is widespread and deep-seated unrest—from whatever cause—there will be crime, delinquency, riots, and disrespect for law and authority. The American system has been stable because it has been flexible and has adapted to meet the changing needs of each generation. When it does not flex fast enough or meet the challenge, there is a decline in respect for law and order and all hell breaks loose. There is more hell to come.

In 1838, Abraham Lincoln was twenty-eight and a

member of the Illinois State Legislature. The state of mind
of the nation 130 years ago was similar to the state of
mind of the nation today in that there was widespread
lawlessness. Much of the disorder was caused by men
who simply took the law in their own hands to achieve
what they asserted was justice. Lincoln saw no defense
against this lawlessness without a very basic change in the
state of mind of the nation. Here is one paragraph of his
speech 130 years ago:

> Let reverence for the laws be breathed by every Ameri-
> can mother to the lisping baby that prattles on her lap.
> Let it be taught in schools, in seminaries and in colleges.
> Let it be written in primers, spelling books and the
> almanacs. Let it be preached from the pulpit, pro-
> claimed in legislative halls, and enforced in Courts of
> justice. And, in short, let it be the political religion of
> the nation, and let the old and the young, the rich and
> the poor, the grave and the gay, of all sexes and tongues
> and colors and conditions, sacrifice unceasingly upon its
> altars.

The problems of the state of mind of the nation and negative attitudes toward the law are not new. Nor have the
speeches on the subject undergone any improvement in
the past 130 years. It was said then about as well as it
could be said; let's keep saying it! Just saying it, though,
will never solve the major sources of discontent that are
such a catalyst to lawlessness. Lincoln was not elected
President on that speech alone, but because he directed
his attention to all the basic problems of his time.

In the end, however, lawlessness reaches a point where

the issues are spelled out in different terms. At the beginning of an era of lawlessness, the debate concerning how to handle the problem is spelled out in terms of "lives versus property." But as the disorders progress, the pattern of history has been to shift to spelling out the issue in different terms. Less and less, it is "lives versus property," and increasingly the issue is stated in terms of "law versus anarchy." The way the issue is defined will determine in no small degree the method of dealing with the problem. Although there is a great desire on the part of large segments of the public to avoid confronting conditions that are such a catalyst to disorders, there is obviously a mood developing in the nation not to submit to anarchy every weekend. Thus, as the issue shifts from "lives versus property" to "law versus anarchy" there will be a marked change in the method and extent of force used to suppress riots.

However the issue is quite clear, and whatever methods are used to suppress disorders, there can be no successful substitute for wide-sweeping programs that will dissolve some of the major causes of unrest. It is to these programs that the nation must direct its major effort.

In America, each passing year brings deteriorating conditions that in turn give rise to crime, delinquency, and riots

1. *The total number of people in families that have less than the threshold poverty level of living are not decreasing substantially.*

2. *The number of unwanted children being born into*

inadequate homes and families—where they have little chance of developing into normal, productive citizens—is increasing.

3. Although the schools of America are increasing their services, the total demand on the school systems has sky-rocketed, and thus *the schools, from the point of view of fulfilling demands made on them, are in a worse position than ever before in the history of this nation.*

Schools are being asked to provide education for the three out of ten who formerly dropped out before completing high school. They are being asked to educate the borderline psychotic, the mentally retarded, the child from the socially and emotionally deprived home, and so on. At the same time they are being asked to give quality education to every child. Schools of America need 100 per cent more resources to perform the tasks demanded of them.

4. *The leaders of those who mobilize and direct the actions of the discontented have openly advocated lawlessness and violence. They have successfully increased the number of people who have adopted this approach each passing year.* Their leadership and groups are fragmented, but this does not alter the general drift of events. The situation is made more serious because the leadership of the fragmented groups, either contented or discontented, has failed to define specific programs that would greatly alter the lives of millions of people in a manner that would effectively dissolve the conditions that produce the widespread and deep-seated discontent. The fragmented leaders of the discontented are extremely capable men and are being extremely successful in arous-

ing their followers. At the same time, there is a failure to identify specific programs that would sufficiently change the lives of millions of people to effect an ultimate solution.

There are no broad, sweeping programs now being advocated by either major political party or by the leadership of the discontented that will meet the needs of the situation

1. Many of the TAP (Total Action on Poverty) programs are excellent, but if they were increased tenfold they could not reverse the tide of events. Such programs are important, but they should be considered only as aids to more basic far-reaching programs. *For the most part, these programs are better expanded through the school systems than by other units of government.*

2. Improvement in resources for police departments and Courts, and also more resources for rehabilitation of delinquents and adult criminals is essential immediately, without waiting for programs that take years to effect. But, again, this approach without additional programs is as ineffective as trying to bail out the Detroit River with a bucket.

3. There is a failure to treat the problem as though it had the same magnitude of the problem of Vietnam, building expressways, or Social Security with Medicare. Certainly the public is alarmed and concerned, but like America before Pearl Harbor, there are millions of Americans who believe that the problem will not touch them directly, and public officials only express the will of their

constituents when they take the position that the situation will eventually resolve itself by more effective law enforcement and perhaps a few not-too-expensive TAP programs.

The nation is not moving toward a solution of its domestic problems at this time

1. The sense of urgency disappeared from nearly every segment of the nation a few months after the major 1967 riots in Detroit and Newark.

2. A few months after the riots ended, Congress was busy trying to cut programs that were aimed at the heart of the most troubled areas. Neither the Democratic or the Republican party gave sufficient support even to the very inadequate programs that were before Congress in 1967.

3. Even members of Congress who were a few months ago talking about strong antiriot and anticrime legislation now seem to be silent. Even the "get-tough" group is not as vocal. Nor is there any reason to believe that even those who limit their proposals to "support your local police" and the "lock-them-up" approach are really going to do much about getting the police and Courts the much-needed facilities.

4. The public does not want to think about riot problems. I speak before many groups and as a matter of practice have a give-and-take question-and-answer period with the audience. Two months after the riot there ceased to be great interest and there seemed to be a desire not to talk about it.

5. Suburbia does not feel too much involved, and there is a steady trickle out of Detroit to the suburbs of citizens who prefer sending their children to schools outside the city. This is not dramatic, but over a period of time it represents a considerable factor. A survey will undoubtedly show that a sizable number of the students that the Detroit School Board could not find when school opened this fall are now enrolled in schools in communities outside Detroit.

6. Crime, delinquency, and riots may well be the major issue in the 1968 elections. Yet it is very possible that, regardless of the outcome, no effective steps will be taken to reduce or solve the problems that command the focus of attention of the nation.

The situation confronting America is far more complex than listing some of its major woes. It cannot be fairly presented by ignoring some of the very substantial progress that is being made in the lives of the vast majority of Americans. It is paradoxical that the great progress of America aids in bringing about the great cleavage and unrest among those who are being left behind and outside the mainstream

1. The sum total of educational progress of the nation is astounding. The juveniles of today are becoming the best-educated and best-informed generation that ever walked this earth, and their achievements will dwarf the achievements of their parents. But the problem of the dropouts will also dwarf the domestic problems that confronted former generations.

2. There is an immense amount of money being spent by federal, state, and local governments to help people. The federal government alone spends $25 billion a year on welfare, social security, education, and programs designed to help people in lower income brackets. The nation is making a major effort to assist all its citizens.

3. There is an expanding economy and more opportunity in the nation for its citizens than ever before in history. Business and industry more than ever before have an eye open for assisting and placing the hard-to-place worker.

Why the paradox? Why, if the nation is strengthening its fabric, do conditions deteriorate and produce crime, delinquency, and riots? There are many reasons; here are a few:

1. The greater the nation's prosperity, the greater the cleavage between the "have-nots" and the "haves"—and the greater the discontent, the frustration, the bitterness, and the unrest.

2. Yesterday's poverty was respectable and produced an Abraham Lincoln. Today's poverty produces a *poverty of spirit* as well as stigma, despair, rebellion, defeat, anger, futility, and failure. The communications media portray the affluence of the majority to those living in poverty on a minute-by-minute basis. The message of affluent America goes directly into millions of poverty homes in the most effective way that the best minds in the advertising business can devise.

3. Millions of Americans have been sold on the middle-class way of living before they can possibly afford it. A

dollar-down, dollar-a-week television set creates desires in millions of Americans below threshold poverty level for things they (and, indeed, the majority) cannot afford. Every five or ten minutes there is a clever ad creating desires for cars, modern homes, clothes they simply cannot afford. Is anyone fool enough to contend that some of the best minds in the nation, working for high salaries, are failures in creating wants and desires when they are spending hundreds of millions on a medium that goes into nearly every home in the nation? The distorted vision of superaffluent America is being piped into most of the poverty-stricken homes of the nation every five minutes.

It serves no useful purpose to argue that if people can get a television set on any basis they should not complain about their lot. The fact is that millions of Americans now feel stigmatized because they are out of the mainstream of American life. A generation ago the expression "poor but honest" was commonplace. The expression is not in use today, even though millions are "poor but honest." Poverty has lost its respectability, and the poor know it. Today it would be more accurate if we were to say "poor but angry."

Is anyone fool enough to believe that the sixteen-year-old boy in the slum area, with no father and a mother on ADC (Aid to Dependent Children), does not develop a great craving to drive a car? Stolen cars have now reached more than 500,000 a year, and most of them are stolen by juveniles—but very few are boys from two-car homes. The point is not less valid even though car theft is on the rise in families that have one car. Obviously to eliminate poverty will not eliminate crime, but will reduce crime substantially.

4. Many doors to success and normal living have been slammed shut in America. This generation must pass through the school door in order to find successful normal living. The school dropout is in serious trouble. There will be 8,000,000 in the next ten years, a few more than our system can absorb without a great deal of crime, delinquency, and hell-raising. Many will work their way through to normal living, but millions of school dropouts will never be normal, achieving citizens. This identifies about nine-tenths of the problem. In former generations, lack of schooling was not a barrier to successful normal living.

5. The *unwanted child* does not make the grade, whether in the slum areas or in middle-class homes. The emotional qualities of a home are quite as important as the physical qualities. The unwanted child develops emotional problems and winds up outside school and often in Court. There are few acceptable solutions outside the school doors in today's world. Lack of education will soon be as crippling to a person as loss of an arm. But the situation cannot be fully explained in terms of poverty, dropouts, or unwanted children. The climate of lawlessness is also an important factor.

6. There has been created a climate that excuses and even encourages lawless acts with the assertion that many are so situated or oppressed that lawlessness is justified. Nonsense! A large percentage of juveniles caught up in Detroit's riot came from home-owning parents (see Appendix I, page 119). Most of their fathers were working. Many juveniles had summer jobs themselves and were in school with every prospect of keeping in the mainstream of American life. With a breakdown of law and order, the

desire to loot took over, as it always has in every situation of emergency—such as flood, fire, and the like. Most of the juveniles had never been in Court before. However, opposed to this picture is the fact that the day-to-day work of the Court is dealing with low achievers—either dropouts or soon-to-be dropouts. *The riot was very different from the day-to-day caseload of the Court.* It started in the poverty area, but with a complete breakdown of law and order. Many normally law-abiding citizens became involved in looting.

There is no possible way to capsule neatly the complex situation that confronts America. Any person with a fair degree of competence, depending on his political and social views, can select any number of compelling facts and arguments and with perfect logic proceed along to the grand fallacy. I reach most of my conclusions from the major premise that there must be massive changes in the home and school environments of millions of children. If this premise is wrong, then the conclusions have no substance.

The discontented cover a broad spectrum of American life, but the sector of American life that gives impetus to the entire movement is the poverty sector. Urged on by many forces from without as well as within, this sector has provided the sinew and momentum for a large force of discontented that are gradually moving on a collision course with the majority who are in the mainstream of American life.

It is nonsense to attempt to analyze the situation and reach sound conclusions solely on the basis of what percentage of rioters have jobs, etc. The normally law-abiding individual who is caught up in the excitement of the riot and loots is much easier for the police to arrest than the case-hardened professional. Very few fire-setters were apprehended. There is a bill in the Michigan legislature for special penalties for sniping, but few snipers were apprehended. The action clearly starts in the poverty and high-crime-rate areas; these areas present the greatest potential for riots and crime.

Riots and crime are the purulence that comes to the surface from the infection that is increasing beneath the surface. We must and can keep the symptoms (riots and crimes) under control through more effective law enforcement. But more effective law enforcement will do nothing to stop the basic infection, and such measures will have nothing to do with shaping the kind of world in which our children will live out their lives. More basic, far-reaching changes must occur before the infection is dissipated.

There are some similarities between the America of the 1840s to 1850s and the America of today. In pre-Civil War America, it was apparent that powerful forces were moving on a collision course. Historians are still arguing about the causes of the Civil War, but there is no dispute about what actually occurred. There are a multitude of factors in the present situation about which informed men differ, but those differences must not block effective action to dissipate the chief source of the discontent. We simply cannot successfully deflect these forces from a collision course. The only solution is to dissolve and dissipate the chief sources of discontent by absorption into the mainstream of American life. We have the resources. It is a question of priorities.

If we act now, in a decade the greater part of the inflamation can be eliminated. All of it may never be eliminated. We are making the decisions now that will decide the kind of world in which our children will live. Not to act decisively is equivalent to making a decision. If you are drifting down the Detroit River and debating whether to get off at the foot of Woodward Avenue and the debate continues, the river and time will make the decision. You may be past the point where you can effectively carry out your decision. We don't have forever.

Putting a man on the moon is a wonderful achievement for any generation, but this will not be the determining factor in the kind of world we will pass on to our children. This nation has a problem in its own back yard that is spilling over everywhere. Unless we act decisively and promptly, we are very apt to go down in history as the "blundering generation."

In seeking solutions, we may well find it necessary to more than double the $25 billion the federal government is now spending to help its citizens. It will be necessary to promote programs that will substantially change the home and school environments of millions of juveniles.

There is nothing about the present situation that is insurmountable. Other generations of Americans have faced situations that presented even greater challenges, considering the resources available to them. One of the difficulties that limits effective action is the complexity of the present situation. *"If the trumpet gives an uncertain sound, who will obey?"* In our present season of discontent there are a thousand trumpets that call to follow objectives that are too limited in their nature to effect any solution of basic problems. Seldom has there been so much furor with such a total lack of defining goals that could ultimately dissolve the major sources of discontent.

There are many causes of crime, delinquency, riots, and deep-seated discontent. Little purpose is served by enumerating them. Let us approach the problem from another perspective. Let us ask ourselves what kind of country we would like the coming generations to enjoy. If we approach the matter from this perspective, we are less likely to become lost in the maze of causes of our present difficulties. We will be better able to define the course of action we must take. Certainly we would desire a nation where the focal point of effort and attention is *the achievement of its citizens and not the behavior problems of its citizens*. Behavior is at its best when it is a by-product of doing something constructive. *Let us do those things now which will bring about the greatest level of achievement of every citizen in the next generation.*

There are six things that we should do:

1. Support the programs for the police and the rehabilitation programs of the Courts so that we do not become overwhelmed by the rising tide of crime, delinquency, and riots. Law and order must be maintained and law-enforcing agencies must be given many additional tools to do their task until the long-range programs resolve some of the major causes of our difficulties. The necessary tools do not relate to passing laws but rather more police, racial balance in police departments, more facilities for Courts, intensive in-service training courses for both police and Court personnel, and similar programs.

2. Support programs that would bring families up to the threshold poverty level of income. A combination family allowance and negative income tax program are a must.

3. Support programs that would result in effective family planning and reduce the number of unwanted children being born into homes where they have little chance to develop into normal, achieving citizens.

4. Support programs that would give the schools of America from 75 to 100 per cent more resources, so they can give every child in America a quality education and at the same time perform the task never before demanded of any school system in the history of mankind—educating the three out of ten who drop out before completing high school. Schools must have resources to teach the mentally defective, the mentally retarded, the borderline psychotic, the child from the socially and economically deprived home, the unmotivated. At the same time they must improve their standards of education until every child in every school has quality education.

5. Business, industry, and private foundations must get into the business of making productive citizens out of individuals who are now a burden to everyone.

6. Action must be taken for progress and for the conservation of American institutions. Herein lies the common ground for conservatives, moderates, and liberals. The sixth imperative is to understand and to act.

These six proposals are very much interrelated. The number of programs that would change the lives of millions of children are limited. It is not such a difficult task to measure those proposals against other possibilities for producing mass changes in the lives of millions of people. Obviously, to be effective, programs must directly affect millions and they must make some very substantial changes in either home or school environments. *Where but the home and the school is there any real possibility of making any major changes in the lives of millions of children?*

One important footnote should be made concerning the assertion that home and school offer the major areas where effective changes can be made. Delinquent acts of juveniles usually occur when juveniles are properly on leisure time but not using it correctly. One major objective of our school system should be to teach people how to use leisure time. Of course, there must also be facilities for people to use leisure time. Good recreation centers, with attractive programs available to every child and adult in urban areas, are a must. The teaching of hobbies must become a substantial part of education of juveniles. *Boredom is a major factor in delinquency, discontent, and rebellion.* It is one of the major causes of car thefts by juveniles from depressed homes. Nearly all of the major riots in the nation have been triggered by events that rose out of the way in which people spend their leisure time in depressed areas. Their rebellion against police interference in their choice of leisure activities is too well known to discuss. Twelfth Street boasts no members in the Detroit Yacht Club, nor can residents legally drink after hours. That blind pig on Twelfth Street was their club. One riot in this nation was triggered by attempts of the authorities to turn off a fire hydrant that the people in the area had opened on a hot day. This was their swimming pool.

If the police let the blind pigs operate, they will be accused of taking graft or not doing their duty. There may have been good reason to turn off the fire hydrant. If the habit of letting fire hydrants replace swimming pools was permitted to spread, it could lower water pressure to the point of creating fire hazards. Would it be too simple for someone to start a private club on Twelfth Street so that drinking could legally be permitted after hours? Would it be too simple to build swimming pools so that it would not be necessary to open fire hydrants as a substitute?

But let us return to the subject of schools. Schools are going to have to adjust in many ways to fit the needs of today's world. *They are going to have to spend much more effort teaching people how to use leisure time. They are going to have to give mandatory courses in family living, starting in grade school and continuing on in high school. These courses must include sex education. There must also be massive adjustments in the educational system to better meet the needs of the three out of ten who are dropping out before they graduate from high school. In order for any educational program to be successful in depressed or slum areas, curricula for training schoolteachers must give these teachers an awareness of problems that confront these families. In every curriculum for teacher preparation there should be courses of exposure that bring the practice teacher not only to the school situation but also to the neighborhood and its very different set of problems.*

The most effective way to reduce race problems is not to treat these problems as race problems but to effect basic changes in the home and schools of millions of children of all races.

The extremists among the whites who believe that the situation can be resolved only by force offer no solution whatsoever. There must be more effective law enforcement, but to rely solely on law enforcement methods, without broad programs that will reduce the steam in the kettle, will ultimately result in greater explosions.

The extremists among the Negroes who believe that the solution to their problems lies in force offer no solution. Like white extremists, they would lead all of us down a bloody road to nowhere.

The cry of the Negro is for acceptance and dignity. The middle-class and professional Negro will ask how these proposals will change their situation. *The answer is simply that no minority race ever achieved full acceptance until, as a group, it reached the equivalent educational level and earning power of the rest of the population.*

There are as many whites living in poverty as there are Negroes. There are at least four times as many whites as Negroes, and thus the percentage of Negroes living in poverty is far greater than the per cent of whites living in poverty. *Programs to abolish poverty should be directed at all races.* But the point that must be stated in the strongest terms is that such a high percentage of Negroes living in poverty and such a high percentage having a low educational level creates a very difficult situation for middle-class and professional Negroes. It is a situation that must be greatly changed before there can be any real solution to race problems.

There was never full acceptance of the Irish, the Italians, or other immigrants until their earning power and educational level *as a group* came in line with the majority of the population. At that point, acceptance came to them. One of Irish lineage was elected President. In the memory of some now living, there were signs in businesses in some sections of the nation that read "JOB VACANCIES! IRISH NEED NOT APPLY!" *The conditions precedent to full acceptance was educational and earning equivalent to the groups around them. Nor did they have to wait for all of their group to reach an acceptable level before full acceptance by majority groups. The fact that there is such a high percentage of Negroes living in poverty and such a high percentage with low educational levels creates impossible roadblocks to full acceptance and dignity for middle-class and professional Negroes.*

The impact on attitudes of all races toward the large number of Negroes living in slums is apparent. A very sizable number of Negro schoolteachers do not care to teach in slum schools. This is understandable, for many of them fought their way out in order to get into the professional class. The whites have equivalent attitudes toward the poverty areas of their *own race*. The reaction of Negroes and whites are identical toward these similar situations. *However, white minority groups are no longer confronted with the high percentage of their group living under these conditions, and therefore are not confronted with the same roadblocks to acceptance and dignity that confront middle-class and professional Negroes.*

These roadblocks to acceptance and dignity must be cleared away. *An all-out undertaking to clear them away will, in itself, result in a marked shift in attitude among both Negroes and whites.*

What explanation can be given for the fact that thousands of middle-class Negroes became involved in looting in the July riot?

1. Whenever there is a breakdown of law and order, some people who are normally law-abiding will loot. This has happened in cases of fire, flood, and the like, regardless of race.

2. In the July riot, the whites tended to think that the thrust of the riot was against whites as individuals and therefore stayed home. Those who did go out were welcomed and looted alongside Negroes.

3. *That there is considerable resentment among middle-class and professional Negroes because of the failure to receive full acceptance from the white community. This resentment was a considerable factor in the number of middle-class Negroes who became involved in looting.*

4. The situation of the middle-class and professional Negro is complicated by the fact that the extremists in their own race are hostile toward them. They are in the middle in more ways than one.

I have heard debates about whether or not the July riot was a race riot. If it was not a race riot, it will do until one comes along. It is impossible to effect far-reaching programs for one race and not apply the same programs to all races. The programs advocated here would be directed at about 60 per cent white and 40 per cent Negro. This includes both poverty and birth control programs. Give or take 10 per cent either way, it makes no difference in the ultimate solution. *But there must be a marked shift in priorities as to the manner in which the nation is directing its energies and wealth in order to undertake effective programs.*

The race problem is therefore effectively dealt with by these proposals. It is only by broad programs that apply to all races that any reasonable solution to the race problems in America will ever be effected.

Everyone looks out at the world through his own window. The view is different for each of us. I look at it from the viewpoint of a Juvenile Court Judge of a jurisdiction of nearly 2,800,000 people of all races and economic levels. The jurisdiction contains at least 400,000 people in depressed economic conditions. During my seven years on the bench I have observed a parade of cases of delinquent, as well as neglected, children. There is no end to it, and in spite of all present programs the problems are increasing. All the gimmicks have been tried and found wanting. There are no quick or easy solutions. The problems are not going to go away by themselves.

I do not expect that all of my proposals will be accepted with any widespread enthusiasm; I came to accept two of these proposals myself only within the past few years. The thought of *extending welfare programs* is obnoxious to an ex-farm boy who was raised with some very strong beliefs concerning self-reliance even when wheat was forty cents a bushel. I have little enthusiasm about this particular proposal. It is made because it is *absolutely necessary* and the alternative of not doing it is equally obnoxious and *far more devastating*.

Professors and research experts could undoubtedly do a much better job in presenting these proposals. They are being presented more from the point of how and why I came to embrace them than by accumulating data to support conclusions already reached. And, as long as I am taking the "testimonial approach," I might as well be completely honest. I have supported a number of sweeping programs in my lifetime that did not turn out as I expected.

1. *Public Housing*: I was a strong supporter of public housing during the five and one-half years I served on Detroit's Common Council. At that time, I believed that proper housing by itself would effect a reduction of crime and delinquency. It won't. Providing suitable structures or homes for thousands of people through public housing has not been such a controlling factor in their lives that it has reduced crime, delinquency, or welfare in the slightest degree. If you are a nonswimmer in ten feet of water and the water level is lowered to nine feet, it makes no difference; you still drown. There must be changes other than housing for public housing to be effective, but this does not refute the necessity for more housing. However, to rely on housing in itself as a condition that will greatly change the behavior of people is futility. Proper housing will nevertheless create a more suitable setting in which to effect more basic changes.

2. I was raised on an eighty-acre farm during the depression years. I (and my father, who was Commissioner of Agriculture for the State of Michigan) supported broad sweeping programs of federal assistance directed at saving the family farm or small farmer.

As it turned out, all the programs in the world could not save the small farmer, because changes in methods of farming made it impossible for the family or small farmer to survive. Thus, the chief objective for supporting the programs could not be achieved and the small farmer has been phased nearly out of existence.

3. Social Security did achieve its objective and has substantially changed the lives of millions of Americans for the better. Thirty years ago (1937), Social Security was being referred to as the Dog Tag Law.

Two out of three of the broad programs I have supported during my lifetime did not achieve their hoped-for objective. But this did not mean that they failed or that I would not again support them. They did accomplish much good. But I now tend to look at sweeping proposals with an eye of a skeptic and it took me a long time to "grow into" at least two of these proposals. I can therefore reasonably expect most people to reject one or more of the proposals at this time. But events carry their own logic.

Time and circumstances will force acceptance of these proposals. The time is not yet: There are too many million Americans who believe, as millions did before Pearl Harbor, that somehow the problem would not touch them personally. They are wrong. Crime, delinquency, and riots are symptoms of a condition that will eventually touch every American. It is *important* to treat the symptoms. It is *vital* to treat the conditions that produce the symptoms.

As a group these proposals would make substantial changes in the lives of millions of Americans. Put into effect, these proposals would bring returns for money and effort expended a hundredfold in law-abiding, achieving citizens within a generation.

The first imperative: There must be more vigorous law enforcement

There must be an immediate and substantial increase in the resources of police, courts, and rehabilitative institutions in order to maintain law and order.

A. Recent Supreme Court decisions make it necessary for police to establish many cases by evidence other than the statements of the accused. This does not create the handicap to successful prosecution of cases that was first feared by many. It now takes more police time to obtain evidence to establish cases. This is so apparent to a trial Judge that no proof of the assertion is offered. It is equally apparent that the police must be more skilled to work effectively within the present legal framework. But it can be done! All this adds up to the fact that Detroit could use 50 per cent more police. Furthermore, if the police are going to be skilled enough to work effectively, then they must be classed as highly skilled workers and given better preparation to be more effective patrolmen. *Highly skilled workers come high. Higher pay and more policemen are absolutely essential to more effective law enforcement.* This is true everywhere in the nation.

There must be police racial balance. One of the prime objectives of police departments must be to recruit Negroes.

B. Juvenile Courts have lost a good deal of public confidence because they have not had the tools to do their jobs. Unfortunately, some of the citizens who will complain about a Judge turning juveniles loose when they should be detained will also vote against furnishing the Court the facilities necessary to detain them. Juvenile Courts throughout the nation need more Youth Home space, more Training School space, and more probation officers.

There is not the slightest doubt in my mind that Juvenile Courts are going to remain woefully short of necessary rehabilitative institutions for many years to come. They will also continue to be short of probation officers. The Wayne County Juvenile Court has one probation officer for every 8000 children of school age, not a very promising situation for curbing delinquency in Wayne County.

In the long run, the important things that have to do with eliminating crime or juvenile delinquency have the least to do with institutions that confine either adult prisoners or juveniles. These institutions are a last resort and are monuments to our failures. In 1965 the State Training Schools admitted an additional 200 boys from Wayne County as compared to 1964. Records of the Detroit Police Department show that the rate of delinquents returned to Court for additional trouble dropped 22 per cent in one year. Quite a record for Juvenile Court! Except that there was one small note of warning. The total amount of delinquency went up in 1965 even though recidivism of delinquents went down. The rise in number of first offenders was continuing. So all the additional Training School space did was *decrease the rate of the increase of delinquency* in Wayne County. This is important, for this must be done, if we are not to be overrun by crime and delinquency.

C. The institution most needed by Wayne County Juvenile Court at this time is a *combination Youth Home and short-term rehabilitation center* for delinquents. The present Youth Home has a rated capacity of 160 boys and 60 girls, far short of the needs of a County of approximately 2,800,000 population. Wayne County faces serious revenue problems; it is unlikely that the much-needed facility will be available for at least five years. If we had the necessary building it would remain empty because of lack of money to operate it. The present orders to the Wayne County Juvenile Court are to cut $114,000 from the Court budget and $35,000 from the Youth Home budget. The orders are to go backward, not forward.

Juvenile Courts must have a vast increase in resources and more probation officers to be effective.

During this season of unrest and violence one should offer total support to giving the police and the Courts the necessary tools to see that this nation is not overrun by delinquency, crime, and riots. Law and order must be maintained by every proper means necessary; this includes confinement in institutions for law violators. At the same time, confinement of law violators will never solve the deep-seated unrest in this nation. To provide the police and courts with more facilities and to stop there is futile. There must be programs that will make substantial changes in the home and school environment of millions of juveniles before there will be any real solution to our problems.

The second imperative: There must be a substantial reduction, through birth control and family planning, in the millions of unwanted children now being born to parents who are not likely to provide the care necessary for them to develop normally in their homes

1. The *unwanted child* can be born into any home, regardless of income, race, or neighborhood.

Example No. 1: Children born in a home where parents could easily provide for the physical needs of children.

Recently before me was a case on a neglect petition where the parents had repeatedly broken the arms and legs, and also fractured the skull, of a child under four years of age. Another child in this family was found dead in the crib at the age of one month. The mother is now pregnant again.

There is a steady stream of child-abuse cases coming into the hospitals and Courts. It is apparent that many deaths of young children by abuse are still listed as accidental deaths. It is next to impossible to prove most cases beyond a reasonable doubt when the child is dead or too young to talk. Many cases of child abuse involving broken bones are admitted by parents in Juvenile Court and the child is removed from the home. The circumstances are such that the parents could never be charged with a crime, for in the criminal court all they would need to do is remain silent and abuse by any one person could not be proven.

It is very possible that the main cause of death of children under four years of age is abuse by parents. Child abuse is widespread and not restricted to any racial or economic group. This is not to contend that a greater percentage of parents are abusing their children than in former generations. Doctors and Courts are learning to identify by the hundreds child-abuse cases that were called accidents even five years ago. The abused child represents the extreme case of the unwanted child. They were unwanted at the time of birth and are held captive in an environment that makes Dante's Inferno a picnic by comparison.

Example No. 2: Also recently before me on a neglect petition was the case of an unmarried mother who had thirteen children by various men. One of her unmarried daughters had already had three children and another unmarried daughter two. One sixteen-year-old daughter is pregnant. We are now into the third generation of illegitimacy, delinquency, and welfare and there has been no program that would bring about a substantial environment change in any one of three generations.

2. For the past seven years I have witnessed a constant stream of children before my Court, on either delinquency or neglect petitions, from every walk of life, who were just simply unwanted children in homes in which they could not develop normally. The rejection takes many forms, but it all adds up to the same thing: *unwanted children.*

3. *The social-work approach will never solve more than a small portion of the problem.*

There will never be enough social workers even to begin to solve the problem of inadequate homes—homes in which a child cannot develop normally. For every child that is saved by the special services of social workers there will be a hundred more born in similar circumstances who will need special services in order to develop into normal, useful citizens. The social-work approach has produced many outstanding results for particular individuals, but the battle was lost before it began in the attempt to reduce the sum total of our social problems by making the social-work approach the focal point of the attack.

4. *The problem presented by unwanted children in homes where they cannot develop normally is a vastly different problem from what it was generations ago, and the results are different.*

Children are no longer economic assets to parents and they do not work in shops or factories at an early age. Mandatory educational requirements are greater and child labor laws are stricter. Former generations had a cruel solution to the problem of the uneducated, emotionally disturbed, or unwanted child. They labored at tasks beyond their maturity and many were simply worked to death. One solution to these problems today is also cruel. The demand on every child today is for education. *Unwanted and poorly cared-for children do not learn well in today's world. They fail in the one area that offers them hope to work through to normal living—success in school. They end up out of school,* in Court, in detention homes, in jails, on welfare, and generally a burden on everyone else. Unwanted children in homes where they cannot succeed or develop normally is just another way of saying crime, delinquency, riots, welfare, etc. The children who are Court wards in Wayne County on neglect petitions have suffered quite as much from emotional neglect as from physical neglect when they were with their parents. In today's world it takes something more than food, clothing, and shelter to produce a normal, achieving child. There is no way to furnish it if the nation is going on producing millions of unwanted children.

5. Up to the present time, family planning and birth control programs have failed to make a sizable impact on the problems in the United States.

   A. The Planned Parenthood Leagues do an excellent job within their resources.

   B. Government at every level has gradually moved over in the past decade from undercover approval to *limited* positive open support; but because it is still very difficult to be a statesman out of office, most elected officials support birth control programs *"to some extent, that is; more or less, that is; to some degree, that is."*

   C. Thus a situation exists where it is possible for the local communities, although supplied with federal funds for the purpose, to take little if any effective action to initiate birth control programs.

6. *What are some factors that would lead to more effective birth control programs?*

   A. Birth control practices should not be forced on

anyone. The attempt to take away the freedom of choice raises issues that retard the whole program. The issue of free choice of birth control methods must at all times be kept separate from the issues raised by abortion or forced birth control. The unwise approach of confusing these issues opens a controversy to which there can be no reasonable solution.

B. The federal government not only should make unlimited funds available for birth control programs at local levels, but funds should also be available for a variety of programs or means of selling a program. It is possible that, in the end, a federal agency itself will have to operate the programs. Hopefully, this need not occur.

C. There must be strong, clear public statements by as many people as possible, including public officials, that they actually support government-sponsored programs for birth control that permit freedom of choice of the individual. Public officials must sponsor and vote for a variety of effective programs.

There will be little decrease in crime, delinquency, riots, or welfare problems until there is a substantial reduction in the number of unwanted children born into homes where they will not develop into normal, law-abiding, productive, citizens. The season of our turmoil will continue, for the time is not yet when effective action will be taken.

The third imperative: this nation must adopt a family allowance program similar to Canada's program, or the nation must accept the inevitable consequences resulting from having millions of children raised in homes with incomes below or near threshold poverty level

Failure to act spells underachieving children, more school dropouts, crime, delinquency, riots, and problems that tend to increase in geometric proportions.

1. *What is the extent and number of children living in homes below the threshold of poverty level income?*

A. The criteria used to define threshold poverty is a family unit of four with an income of less than $3335 per year. Using this criterion, there are millions of children in poverty homes. However, there are millions of additional children in homes that fall in the income between poverty level and middle-class income. Certainly, there are millions of children who need help and are above the poverty level but below middle-class income level.

B. Millions in the poverty level are living far below the threshold level of poverty criteria, $3335 for a family unit of four is far above the income level of homes in which millions of children are living today.

C. We must face the fact that well over ten million children in the most affluent nation of the world need help. Unbelievable when one considers that sixty-two nations of the world have some sort of family allowance program! We have sent some of these nations foreign aid; this helps put them into a position to give family allowances. *It's time we looked after our own, as well.*

D. Present welfare and other government programs do not help more than one-third of the children who need help. Furthermore, the family allowance program is not degrading, does not discourage work or initative or have the evils of many of the present welfare programs. No wonder sixty-two nations have adopted it.

E. There is nothing about the family allowance program which is proposed that would result in more children being born. It will pay a fraction of the cost of raising a child and dull the sharp edges of poverty. This is important and must be done.

2. *How much should be paid for each child?*

A. Canada pays as follows:

1. Up to age 10 $ 6 per month
2. Ages 10 to 15 $ 8 per month
3. Ages 16 to 17 (in school) $10 per month

B. The United States should double the rates paid in Canada. That would be $240 a year for the sixteen-year-old, which would be the highest rate.

3. *What countries now have a family allowance program?*

A. There are sixty-two. Australia, Canada, Denmark, Finland, West Germany, East Germany, Iceland, Ireland, Netherlands, New Zealand, Sweden, the USSR, and the United Kingdom are the countries that pay to all families.

4. *Why should a taxpayer who has, through his own efforts, worked his way up from poverty and provided his own family a good home, now support a program where he would be taxed to help a family where the parents may have put forth only a minimal effort to help themselves?*

A. I would have opposed a family allowance a few years ago because I could find no satisfactory answer to this question. However, the steady stream of neglected children that come to the Wayne County Juvenile Court have, over a period of years, provided me a complete answer. Not a single one of these children were responsible for having inadequate parents. *The burden of poverty falls on the children, and they did not choose their parents.*

It was also apparent that many of these parents were trying as hard as they could to provide for their families. Many did their best but were inadequate to cope with the problems that confronted them.

B. Children are failing in these homes and it does not do a single thing to correct the problem by fixing blame. There are always going to be freeloaders, but the object is to create a situation where we develop as many responsible, achieving citizens as possible. This means doing something for children in poverty homes in the United States, as well as sending foreign aid to other countries that have family allowances for their children.

5. *The family allowance should be paid for every child in the United States regardless of the income of the family*

A. That is the way it is done in Canada, and it saves hiring an army of employees to determine who is cheating.

B. The ones in the higher income brackets will pay it back in taxes anyway. Residence should be the only requirement.

If any attempt is made to make a cut-off point on income, it becomes necessary to make many adjustments because a host of problems present themselves. Pay it to everyone and if they don't want it, let them deduct the sum due them from the sum due the government on their income tax. That would cut cost of administration.

6. *Would the family allowance make any real difference since it only pays a fraction of the cost of raising a child?*

A. It would make a great difference. Even busfare home from Court is an item for many that come to Juvenile Court on neglect petitions.

B. *The family allowance is the program that puts money where it really counts.* A large percentage of poverty families have a large number of children. The families in which there are no male adults in the home are at the lowest poverty level. A family allowance program is a Social Security program for children, and it is needed even more than the Social Security program for adults. It is inconceivable that the most affluent nation in the world can afford everything under the sun except to care for its children. *Children living in poverty are not responsible for their situation.*

A negative income tax plan would be another way of

attacking the problem. Both the negative income tax plan and family allowance plan have advantages and disadvantages. The negative income tax plan would be better for many families below threshold poverty but would do nothing for millions near or slightly over threshold poverty. *A combination of the two plans would, of course, be the best answer.* Adopt the family allowance plan at the same level as Canada and apply it across the board to people in every income bracket. Then adopt a negative income tax plan that would bring every family up to threshold poverty, regardless of whether children are in the home or not. Of course, payment made to a family under the family allowance plan would be considered in determining whether or not a family was below threshold poverty. There would not be a "double dip" by those below threshold poverty if the combination plan were adopted.

On November 30, 1967, the Ford Motor Car Company issued the text of a speech by Mr. Arjay Miller, its President, in which Mr. Miller advocated a negative income tax program. A generation ago, millions thought that Henry Ford was insane when he started paying $5 a day to the workers of Ford Motor Company. This is not the first time leadership has come from Ford Motor Company in grasping what has to be done to change the face of America. *Mr. Miller says the negative income tax can work so that it does preserve incentives to those able to work, that it can be efficient in getting money to those only in need, and that it would be efficient to operate.*

Here is one example of how a negative income tax plan might work: Set the threshold poverty level at $3,335 for a family of four—adjusted up and down depending on the size of the family unit. In a family unit of four the total income for the year is $2800. At the time the income tax return is made, the federal government sends a check for $535, which would bring the family up to a total income of $3335 or threshold poverty level.

Very few people want to live at threshold poverty level. The family allowance has not been any major factor in deterring initiative in Canada or 61 other nations. Neither would a negative income tax, or a combination of both programs.

The writer wishes to again refer to the speech made by Mr. Arjay Miller, President, Ford Motor Company on November 30, 1967, in which he advocates a negative income tax as a must for combating poverty. I had to hear thousands of neglect petitions in Juvenile Court before I came to the same general conclusions Mr. Miller reached.

I have accumulated volumes of material concerning poverty problems and proposed solutions, but basically my opinions result from what I have myself observed in the neglect cases that come from poverty homes. Day by day and year by year there pass through the Court an endless parade of cases in which poverty has laid a heavy hand on children who were in no way responsible for choosing their home or environment. I simply grew into the inescapable conclusion that present programs were not effective at all. A new approach is a must.

No one has made a clearer or better statement than Mr. Arjay Miller concerning the *why* and *how* of this new approach. The fact that the statement came from the President of Ford Motor Company surprised me. Mr.

Miller knows more about what must be done than many public officials whose business it is to know. (Mr. Miller's complete statement appears in the Appendix, page 178. Every American should read it; the proposal is worth much more than all the antiriot legislation pending in Congress or in all of the State Legislatures.)

There was a time in the history of mankind when poverty seemed to be a prerequisite for sainthood, but this is not an age of saints. Poverty in America must go—and soon.

The fourth imperative: There must be massive federal aid to education

The resource of the schools must be nearly doubled to insure quality education for every child in America. The following facts have become very clear both at the national and local levels

1. The school offers the most promising opportunity for aiding and making changes in the lives of millions of children through governmental action. There is only one probation officer for every 8,000 children of school age in Wayne County. This figure is true for the rest of the nation. The impact of Courts on the lives of millions is going to be very little compared to that of the schools. A hundred probation officers are not going to have much impact in a county of nearly three million population.

2. The schools are being asked to do a task never before performed in the history of the world: to educate and make useful citizens of the mentally defective, the retarded, the borderline psychotic, the child who has no motivation, and the child that has all sorts of behavior problems.

Many of these juveniles in generations gone by dropped out of school and dug ditches or did similar work. Now ditches are dug by machines.

Under our present economy, there are millions of children dropping out of school who, at best, will never earn more than a marginal living, which will be insufficient to support a family at anything more than poverty level.

It is true that many make a good living without an education. It is also true that school dropouts will constitute nine-tenths of our problems in the next generation, and there are more of them than our system can absorb. There will be eight million dropouts in this nation in the next ten years. Our jails, our Training Schools for delinquents, our Youth Homes, and our welfare rolls are loaded largely with school dropouts and low achievers. A high school diploma is virtually a guarantee against getting locked up.

3. All children, regardless of their achievement level, are entitled to the best education money can buy. The demand of the nation on the schools is to supply quality education for every child. The demand on the schools is not directed solely at the dropout. It is directed at every child in every neighborhood.

There is a limit to which the public will tolerate lowering the educational standards of all in order to give special help to the potential dropouts. The only possible answer is to provide schools with sufficient resources to give every child the best possible education.

Much of the criticism leveled at schools has come about because of the impossibility of their performing the various tasks assigned to them within their limited resources.

The attempt to divide up a scarcity of resources has resulted in an over-all standard of education below that necessary for all children to achieve their full potential. This is not just a slum problem. It is everybody's problem in everybody's neighborhood.

There is something very wrong in a nation that needs to focus so much of its attention on behavior problems of its citizens. Most of us would like to see a time when our attention is directed to the goal of achievement of our citizens rather than their problems of behavior. Today is as good a day as any to begin. Behavior is at its best when it is a by-product of something constructive.

You don't solve problems of crime, delinquency, riots, welfare, etc. You just wear them out.

4. Here is part of a survey furnished by Norman Drachler, Superintendent of Detroit Public Schools:

Estimated Increase in School Support Needed to Provide Quality Education in Detroit in the Next Decade

A. Personnel	
Professionals	$ 601,000,000
Nonprofessionals	227,515,000
B. Books, Supplies, and	
Equipment	236,000,000
C. Nonpublic Schools	
D. Transportation—Enrichment	25,000,000
E. Capital Needs	525,298,900
F. Research and Development—	
Data Processing	
Research and Development	10,000,000
Data Processing	10,000,000
TOTAL FOR 10 YEARS	$1,634,813,900

If the amount were equally divided between each of the ten years, the annual amount would be $163,481,390. The present annual budget for schools, including funds for new buildings, is approximately $170,000,000. Essentially, what this means is that expenditures for schools in Detroit need to be doubled if the City is to provide for its children what schools generally recognize as providing quality education.

Detroit is only used as an example; the problem is national.

There are no programs even contemplated at the national, state, or local level that would begin to answer Detroit's problems, or the nation's, in the field of education. It would be necessary to view the problem nationally as being as urgent and as important as Social Security, with Medicare, expressways, or Vietnam.

The best measure of this or any other generation is how children are prepared to achieve and to live orderly and useful lives. This nation has created an economy and a social system where the doorways to an adjusted, useful life have been slammed shut to those who cannot successfully walk through the school door.

Behavior problems of our citizens will only be solved to the degree that we can get all of our citizens to achieve to their fullest potential. This statement applies in equal force on Twelfth Street in Detroit, in middle-income homes, or in wealthy homes. There is no possible way of solving behavior problems unless the focus of national, state, and local attention is on achievement of children. This can only be done by redirecting billions of additional dollars of the nation's wealth into our schools.

One of the reasons there have been inadequate funds for schools is that those who control the funds at each level of government seem to think that some other level of government ought to contribute more funds. Millages are defeated by voters, and the school boards then turn to the State and federal government for help. Each unit of government looks to some other unit of government for the answer.

Education has become a national problem. Every year thousands of children come from Southern states and enter Michigan schools. If they are not equipped to handle the same level of grade work in Michigan schools, they are all too likely to become dropouts. We have a direct interest in the quality of education being given everywhere. It would take at least $15 billion of federal funds allocated to school districts throughout the nation to bring the national school system up to where it ought to be. This would mean an expenditure of 50 per cent of what Vietnam is costing, and no one at the national level of government is even suggesting such a thing. The state and local governments must increase their contributions to schools.

There will be little chance of decreasing crime rates or delinquency rates, or stopping riots, in the next decade if each year there are tens of thousands of school dropouts not equipped to earn any more than poverty wages, who can never support a family on a middle-class level, and who are no longer really needed in our economic system.

The controlling facts are these:

1. Every child is entitled to quality education; the final solution must be directed at the schools everywhere, not just schools in urban deprived areas;

2. As an emergency measure, more aid should be given immediately to the school problems in high crime rate urban areas;

3. State and local governments need to increase their aid to schools, even though the problem is national in scope;

4. A sizable increase of the nation's resources (at least $15 billion) must be directed into the school systems of the nation in order to insure quality education for every child. In the end this is going to mean massive federal aid to education;

5. The best available means of changing and shaping the lives of millions of juveniles through governmental action lies in the schools of the nation.

The price tag of domestic tranquility can never be less than what it takes to give every child in the nation quality education.

There need be no interference from Washington resulting from a massive federal aid to the education program. Congress can stop this just as easily as they have forbidden interference in the lives of the millions of retired citizens who are on Social Security. Much of the Social Security program comes from the taxpayer, and there is no interference. Why not make it simple? Let the State and local government put up a total of, say, $30 for the education of each child in school. Let the federal government pay the next $400 for each child to the State, which will in turn distribute it on a per capita basis of number of children in school to each school district. *No strings attached!* Detroit is already spending around $500 from various sources for each child. They would easily meet the $300 basic requirement. They would just go on spending the $500 and get the additional $400 federal funds. This would put them about where they should be in order to handle the job. They will need 6200 additional teachers in the next ten years. They could use 250 attendance officers immediately. They need buildings and a host of other things. Schoolteachers must be paid a salary that will attract and keep the male schoolteacher with a family. Too many leave the teaching profession, even though it is their first choice of a career, because of the economic pressure of supporting their families on teachers' salaries. Class sizes, particularly, for the children who are now failing, from whatever cause, are going to have to be cut nearly in half. All this must be done, and at the same time quality education must be available to every child.

Educational Social Security (quality education for every American youth) will be the greatest single factor in determining the kind of America in which our children will live their lives.

Can the nation afford such a program at this time? If $400 cannot be made available to each school district for each child in the district on the basis of residence and enrollment, then let $200 be made available. Millions in federal aid have been given to schools on "hodgepodge" formulas. However, never has the principle been established in federal legislation that would be a commitment to the idea that every American youth must have quality education made available to him.

The federal aid must be distributed across the board without imposing federal regulations, in much the same manner as Social Security payments are made to retired adults.

Let the principle be established now, no matter how puny the beginning. The first step on a thousand-mile journey is unlike any other step in the journey. To take the first step, one must be totally dedicated to do what is necessary to reach the ultimate objective. To establish the principle by Congressional action—to take the first step—is to sound the bugle that will never call retreat.

The fifth imperative: business, industry and private foundations must make a massive effort directed at bringing forth productive citizens of those who, for whatever reasons, are now a burden on their communities

1. *Full-time jobs*: Since the July riots, several auto manufacturing companies have hired from depressed areas.

2. *School-work programs*: There have been a number of programs where the people involved would spend part time in school and part on the job. These programs must be enlarged many times. This calls for joint efforts between the local schools, business, and industry.

3. Jobs alone are not the answer for many who are now unemployed and are making little effort in their own behalf. *Counseling services* on an extensive basis must also

be extended to thousands of individuals, along with the jobs. Job opportunity alone is futile for thousands who must be brought into gainful employment; they also need training and counseling services.

Some special projects in the Detroit area have been successful in bringing people to gainful employment through counseling over an extended period of time. This may even include going to homes and getting the workers out of bed when their supervisor informs the counseling center that they are absent from work. They gradually develop work habits. They improve. It can be made to work. These pilot projects have largely been funded by funds other than business and industry (public funds for the most part).

How far will business and industry go in supplying these additional services themselves? How far will they go in working with some outside agency that is supplying counseling services? Business and industry have not as yet involved themselves in this role to any great degree, but how can the problem be resolved unless they do become deeply involved? To request this of them seems unreasonable—this is not the accepted function of business and industry. But no other solution appears possible. Perhaps private foundations can help private funds and programs to help fill the gap, if industry will cooperate.

It would be pleasant if we could shift some of these necessary programs away from government almost entirely and use the know-how and resources of business, industry, and private foundations.

4. Sooner or later, the time will come when our society will *guarantee employment for all who are willing*

to work. Quite a number of 1967 high school graduates had difficulty finding jobs in Detroit last summer. Some of this was the result of the drive to employ dropouts. Whatever the cause, it makes no difference: *without job opportunities, all else is futile.*

5. Since the 1967 riot, the business community has been loaning some of its brains, experience, and talent to government in the Detroit area. Of course, they have always done this, but the 1967 riot has been a catalyst. The efforts must be expanded in this direction. Also, there are private foundations with hundreds of millions of dollars of resources and a wealth of talent and brains. They also must seek ways to inject themselves more extensively and more effectively into the task of producing citizens who will not be problems.

The sixth imperative: to understand and to act

1. There is a broad spectrum of conservatives, moderates, and liberals who have a common national good will as their objectives. They want to see the American system work. They represent at least 80 per cent of the American people. *Action must be taken for the conservation of American institutions. Herein lie the common grounds for conservatives, moderates, and liberals.* They must recognize and understand the total situation that confronts us. They must sublimate their differences and find common grounds for action.

2. If the great majority of Americans do not unite sufficiently and support far-reaching programs that will make substantial changes in the home and school environments of millions, particularly children, there will be other

summers like 1967 with its riots and its high crime and delinquency rates. This would be the best we could hope for, and as the polarization behind extreme groups continues, there would be even worse to come. Civil war, in the form of repeated and expanded massive civil disturbances, is most likely. This is the avowed objective of leaders of extremist groups. The programs this report advocates would do much to render extremist leadership ineffective. They cannot lead unless they have a large reservoir of extremely discontented people from which to draw their following. Programs that would strike at major sources of discontent are the only way to make extremist leadership ineffective.

3. A considerable number of voices express the view that even to renew present government programs would, in effect, reward the rioters and thus encourage more riots. Obviously, to do nothing would be equivalent to pouring gasoline on the fire, but this particular debate is irrelevant. *With perfect logic one can proceed along to the grand fallacy.* Neither the present "Band-Aid" programs nor the best of logic will alter the situation. There must be sweeping programs that will transcend and alter the basic situation. All else is either inadequate or irrelevant.

It is not contended that the programs herein advocated represent a total solution. These proposed programs are a must in order to reach a solution to move forward and at the same time for America to conserve its basic institutions.

4. Sweeping changes in attitude between the races, and among various economic and social groups, are imperative, but these sorts of changes cannot come about solely by making speeches. To put in effect the programs that

substantially reduce major sources of discontent will, in itself, help bridge the cleavage and promote greater understanding of all but the few who are totally committed to the destruction of American institutions. Obviously, no good can come from building the leadership of persons who are committed to the destruction of basic American institutions or to violence or lawlessness as a means of resolving our problems. Such a course of action will lead not to solutions but to further polarization of extremists and further lawlessness and violence.

5. Very often it is the minority, not the majority, that determines the drift of events in a democracy. It is very clear that in the present solution, the majority opposes the course of action of the extremist groups. However, the majority cannot effectively oppose the minority extremists unless the majority sublimates its differences and unites on programs that will determine the future course of events and shape the America we will pass on to our children.

The greater the challenge, the greater the opportunity. At this point in time, the American people have a magnificent opportunity. The Sixth Imperative, *to understand and to act,* is the yeast that leavens the bread.

When confronted by a long, dangerous, and changing crisis, mankind tends to divide into three main groups

1. *The First Group.* This is the group that will use every means possible to stir the unrest. This group does not necessarily provide direction, but through both lawful and unlawful means seeks to promote greater disturbances.

2. *The Second Group.* This is the group that believes

that the sole way to maintain order is to use greater force. Its members do not direct themselves to attacking the basic causes of the unrest, but rather to suppressing any expression of the unrest by use of force.

3. *The Third Group.*

A. The third group is comprised of all those who do not fall within the first two groups. This group is composed of a broad spectrum of political beliefs and includes *conservatives, liberals, and moderates.* The unifying force within this group is the agreement that the basic problems causing the unrest should be attacked, but there is disagreement as to how it should be done. Within this group, the majority share the beliefs of the second group to the extent that they do not believe that the nation can afford to have anarchy every weekend and that the law must be enforced. But, unlike the second group, the third group would reduce the steam in the kettle by attacking the causes of the unrest. They would not rely solely on force to keep the lid on the kettle, but they would also adopt programs to reduce the steam in the kettle.

B. At the beginning of the crisis and extending over a period of years, the third group is always in the majority. But they will steadily lose ground to the other two groups unless they can unite sufficiently to put into operation effective programs that will reduce the sum total of discontent.

C. *The third group has certain inherent disadvantages in its situation as compared to the first two groups*
(1) The third group is often unable to make as

effective use of the irrational factors of passion and prejudice that play so large a part in determining the course of human events. It is the extreme position that is attractive to those who are moved by the irrational factors.

(2) The third group does not offer the quick solution—which is in fact impossible. However, the third group is constantly under attack by those who promise an immediate solution and who ignore the need for basic changes that would reduce the causes of unrest.

(3) The third group offers a more complex solution, and a considerable portion of mankind demands a simple solution, even when a simple solution is impossible. Many are attracted to the group that promises the simple solution, regardless of the impossibility of performance.

(4) The third group is composed of such a diversity of opinion that it may be incapable of formulating an effective program until it is impelled by such a major crisis that its members unite sufficiently to spell out an effective course of action.

In the present situation in the nation, there will continue to be a polarization around the first two groups for some time to come. The third group cannot help but lose adherents when programs such as Head Start receive rough treatment in Congress. This is a program that should be enlarged tenfold, for it is a program that sets its teeth into the core of the problem. The very considerable troubles that now beset us are nothing to the whirlwinds we will reap unless we promote the programs that will permit these people to succeed in the one area in which they can work their way out of their desperate conditions—school. There is not yet sufficient cohesion and drive in the third group to adopt the far-reaching programs necessary to reduce the steam in the kettle. There is, however, opportunity to make progress at every level, even though the far-reaching programs appear to be unattainable at the present. *At every level of government, we must seek to tailor the present situation rather than wait for the major programs to be adopted. We must be action-oriented at every level* in order to channel and hasten the programs that will surely come, late or soon.

This fall the voters of Wayne County may well have an opportunity to vote on whether they want services reduced in Juvenile Court or whether they want services expanded. In 1967, the Governor of Michigan asked the State Legislature for a special appropriation of $5 million to help give much-needed additional services to schools in depressed areas. The opportunity was there, although not kindly received by the Legislature. There will be other opportunities in 1968. Private industry in the Detroit area is stepping in and providing special job opportunities for those in depressed areas. There will be school millages where the voter can help give the schools the resources to perform their near-impossible task. The opportunity may be presented to voters in some local communities to cast a vote for a larger police force with a salary that will attract and keep a greater number of capable men. The Michigan Legislature can adopt a 75–25 matching fund formula for children in foster homes, as well as a 75–25 matching formula for salaries of probation officers.

It would be the greatest folly to sit back and wait for the broad, sweeping programs that must surely come when so many constructive and positive steps can be taken at every level.

Problems of crime, delinquency, riots, and welfare are not solved: these are problems we just wear out. What we do in the next few years will determine whether we have twenty, ten, five, or one million people in this nation twenty years from now who are a burden to the rest of the nation. If we have twenty million who have not found the way into the mainstream, our children will grow up to live in a nation of turmoil and trouble. If by taking the proper action now we can reduce the number of troubled, noncontributing citizens to under three million, our children will live out their lives in a nation that has its focus of attention on achievement of its citizens and not on the behavior problems of its citizens. It is a question of degree of success or failure, and in the long struggle to produce a nation of law-abiding, achieving citizens there will be no sudden or complete victory. Victory will come with a whisper.

There is no ignoring the fact that the unrest and disturbances that confront the nation extend into many groups, including colleges and hippies. Middle-class mores are under sharp attack, and no one can foresee the extent of the changes that are taking place.

Thousands of these disturbed individuals will undoubtedly follow the same pattern of some individuals I knew at the University of Michigan during the Depression years. Having acquired the responsibility of a home and family, they ended up by voting conservatively, hardly a satisfactory solution to many in the third group. The proposals made here are directed at dissolving the chief source of discontent and trouble within the nation. No attempt has been made to even discuss many of the trouble spots.

"What was, has faded; what now is, shall fade: this is the truth that few beings know"

We must accept the proposition that "only people count" and proceed on the course that will produce a nation of achieving citizens. Then the troubles that confront us will gradually disappear. To achieve this, we must adopt programs that will make massive changes in the home and school environments of millions of children. Hopefully, we will disenthrall ourselves and act before the crisis produces destructive polarization behind extreme groups that can only lead to greater unrest and violence. Hopefully, we will act in time, so that our children can live out their lives in a nation whose attention need not be focused on behavior problems and whose achievements will outshine the achievements of our generation.

Part Four:
Appendix

Appendix I:
Report by Dr. Richard Komisaruk

MEMO TO: Judge Lincoln
FROM: Dr. Komisaruk, Director, Clinic for Child Study
      Wayne County Juvenile Court
DATE: September 13, 1967
RE: *July/67 Riot*

The following is the summary of the first phase of the research on the July riots in which the Clinic has been involved:

1. Attached is a map of which I have fifty copies. Additional copies can be readily processed at the Printing Department of the City-County Building. The map is of a size such that, if folded over, it could be included in a formal report as you requested.

There are several impressions that are conveyed by the map.

    a. The density of pins is not particularly related to the economic class of the neighborhood in which the pins are located. This would suggest that participation in the riots was not necessarily determined by economic factors, an opinion many of us had held.

    b. There is a peculiar paucity of pins in the Hamtramck area, especially in contrast to the area im-

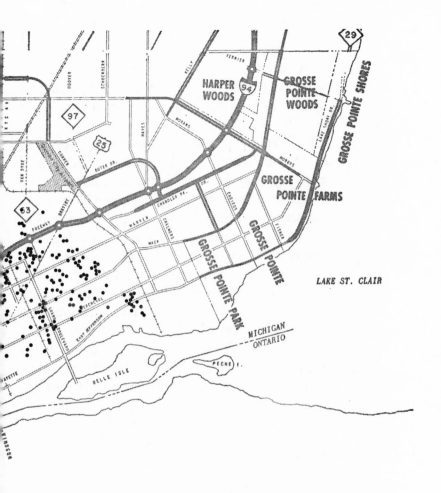

**RESIDENCE LOCATIONS OF ALL
JUVENILES DETAINED IN WAYNE
COUNTY YOUTH HOME JULY 23
THROUGH JULY 28, 1967.**

mediately north of Hamtramck, where there is a dense cluster. Hamtramck should also be compared with Highland Park, where the density of pins seems to be the same as that in contiguous Detroit.

The Negro population of Hamtramck is less than 20 per cent. The percentage of Negro children of school age may be somewhat higher, however. Although there were only four children who reside in Hamtramck arrested, there were thirteen arrests of juveniles in Hamtramck. This suggests a high degree of vigilance on the part of the police there.

It is also my impression that Hamtramck has very much an identity of its own, strongly distinguished from that of Detroit. This is in contrast to Highland Park, which diffuses into Detroit socially and culturally. Thus, youngsters living in Hamtramck might have felt less a part of the riot scene than those immediately to the west and north of them in Detroit.

c. Another area in which there is a sparsity of pins is the downriver area extending from Delray along Fort Street toward Lincoln Park. The Negro population of that area is large. Socially and economically it is certainly comparable to other areas on the map where there is a much greater density of pins.

The area in question is separated from the primary riot area by a strip of territory running from the Detroit River to the Ford Plant, and from approximately the Ambassador Bridge to the Ford Expressway at Livernois. This area, in which there are virtually no pins, is almost exclusively a white neighborhood, although the homes are older and the area is economically similar to the neighboring racially mixed areas. It seems possible that this predominantly white area creates a sort of buffer zone isolating the downriver area from the primary riot disturbance area. It is also possible that other factors affected the downriver community in such a way as to reduce its sense of militancy.

d. The map in the over-all sense demonstrates that youngsters involved in the riot live in areas which follow the course of the spread of the Negro community in the past generation. The 1943 riots were more or less confined to the area now enclosed by the Chrysler, Ford, and Lodge expressways. A substantial part of the Negro community at that time was ghettoized into that area. As the community has spread the feelings and characteristics which make a riot possible have spread with the population. We see then, with the exception of the areas noted above, a diffuse pattern which makes it clear that decentralization of the ghetto alone is not a prophylactic remedy for the outbreak of a riot.

2. After various duplications were eliminated, we found that a total of 673 children were admitted to the Youth Home during the riot. We have broken down these arrests in the following ways: (1) total arrests by precinct of arrest, and (2) total arrests by precinct of residence.

a. Fifty-three children were arrested a significant distance from their homes. The measure of significant distance is that they were arrested more than one precinct away from their home precinct. A breakdown of these precincts of arrest is as follows:

```
Precinct  1 —  15 arrested
          2 —   3     "
          4 —   1     "
          5 —   2     "
          6 —   3     "
          7 —   6     "
         10 —   2     "
         11 —   3     "
         12 —   6     "
         13 —   6     "
         14 —   1     "
         15 —   2     "
         16 —   -     "
Out County —     3     "
                ——
                53
```

b. A corresponding breakdown by precinct of residence is as follows:

```
0 resided in       Precinct       1
2      "               "          2
1      "               "          4
7      "               "          5
2      "               "          6
3      "               "          7
6      "               "         10
5      "               "         11
0      "               "         12
5      "               "         13
1      "               "         14
0      "               "         15
3      "          Highland Park in
18      "          Out County area
——
53
```

c. Two hundred children were arrested outside the precinct in which they live including the contiguous precinct. A breakdown of this by precinct of arrest and precinct of residence is as follows:

27	arrested in	Precinct	1
15	"	"	2
1	"	"	4
16	"	"	5
25	"	"	6
20	"	"	7
16	"	"	10
6	"	"	11
16	"	"	12
18	"	"	13
16	"	"	14
5	"	"	15
1	"	"	16
9	"	Highland Park	
9	"	Hamtramck	
200			

2	resided in	Precinct	1
16	"	"	2
4	"	"	4
16	"	"	5
21	"	"	6
25	"	"	7
42	"	"	10
13	"	"	11
5	"	"	12
18	"	"	13
4	"	"	14
6	"	"	15
18	"	Out County area	
10	"	Highland Park	

200

d. Nineteen youngsters arrested had residence at the time of the riot outside the external boundaries of Detroit (thus excluding Hamtramck and Highland Park). The residences of these children are as follows:

Outside Michigan	4
Ferndale, Michigan	1
Monroe, Michigan	2
Roseville, Michigan	3
Adrian, Michigan (GTS)	1
Washington, Michigan	1
Troy, Michigan	1
Ecorse, Michigan	1
Mount Clemens, Michigan	1
Pontiac, Michigan	1
Inkster, Michigan	2
River Rouge, Michigan	1

19

3. a. The statistical totals regarding age, race, school, grade, and charge had formerly been sent to you. This data is now somewhat revised:

	Boys	Girls
Negro	600	27
White	41	3
Indian	1	–
Mexican	2	–

b. Age distribution pattern reveals the following:

16 years	275	9
15 "	170	7
14 "	95	5
13 "	54	6
12 "	25	1
11 "	15	1
10 "	9	1
9 "	1	0

c. School status of these youngsters is as follows:

	Boys	Girls
12th grade	24	2
11th "	99	3
10th "	122	4
9th "	111	3
8th "	65	8
7th "	44	2
6th "	22	–
5th "	9	–
4th "	11	1
Special Classes	56	3
Boys' Training School	3	GTS 2
Job Corps	1	–
Highland Park College—		
2nd yr.	1	–

	Boys	Girls
Wayne County Training Sch.	–	1
Vista Maria	–	1
Out of School	74	–
Unknown	2	1

    d. As to the charges on which basis they were apprehended, the previous data is essentially correct. Of the 673 charges, the distribution is as follows:

Breaking and Entering	52
Breaking and Entering & Looting	424
Possession of Stolen Property	46
Disturbing the Peace	6
Sodomy	1
Possession of Whiskey	1
Violation of Curfew	75
Inciting to Riot	13
Lodger	3
Possession of Knife	2
UDAA	10
Indecent Liberties	2
Felonious Assault	2
Drunk and Disorderly	2
Robbery—unarmed	2
Assault with intent to murder	2
Reckless Driving	2
Carrying a Concealed Weapon	5
Assault and Unarmed Robbery	2
Attempted Arson	2
Arson	4
	673

The vast majority of these children had had no previous contact with the Juvenile Court. As best we can determine, approximately 500 had never been known to the Juvenile Court prior to their arrest during the riot. Eighty of the youngsters arrested were currently active with the Court at the time of the arrest. About 100 had had previous contact with the Court, but were not currently active on the Court caseload.

4. We are now in the process of doing a more qualitative study of the youngsters, many of whom are being tested by us. Some tentative impressions garnered from this indicates:

a. That 200 of the boys were living with their parents at the time of the arrest, and 248 were living in substitute homes or with one parent. One sixteen-year-old boy was married. This is probably indicative of the trend for the entire 673 cases.

b. About half of the youngsters tested lived in homes which were being purchased by the family.

c. The main source of income for the families of 60 per cent of the youngsters tested was the father. The mother provided the main source of income in 12 per cent, and ADC or other welfare allotments in 19 per cent.

d. Seventy-seven per cent of the youngsters tested have had some sort of job.

e. Forty-one per cent of the boys stated that they had had no police contact prior to the rioting.

SUMMARY

Precinct		Total Arrests by Precinct of Residence	Total Arrests by Precinct of Arrest
Precinct	1	19	44
"	2	84	83
"	4	8	5
"	5	73	73
"	6	59	63
"	7	81	76
"	10	98	72
"	11	29	22
"	12	28	39
"	13	75	75
"	14	21	33
"	15	10	9
"	16	3	4
Highland Park		17	16
Hamtramck		4	13
Out County		18	–
		627	627

MEMO TO: Judge Lincoln

FROM: Dr. Komisaruk

RE: *Official Report on Riot Research Activities* (Supplemental to report of September 13, 1967.)

DATE: May 8, 1968

This memorandum is intended to supplement my earlier communication to you dated September 13, 1967. A sepa-

Re: Official Report on Riot Research Activities

rate memorandum will be issued by Dr. Carpenter describing the final interpretations of the psychological test data.

1. The demographic data are essentially unchanged from the September 13, 1967 report. The interpretation of the material is somewhat different. It is now my impression that the primary reason for the two areas of sparseness on the demographic map is that physical containment in those areas was more effective than in the city at large. This applies particularly to Hamtramck and to that part of the downriver area which was to some extent sequestered by the lifting of the drawbridge on West Fort Street.

2. There seems little question that there was more or less complete and diffuse representation of the entire sociologic and economic span within the black community with respect to participation of these youngsters in the riot activity. To those of us who have participated in the investigation, the clear significance of this is that economic disadvantage was not an exclusive reason for riot activity. The fact that a preponderance of the arrested youngsters were employed (albeit at menial and undesirable jobs) tends to eliminate the unemployment factor as an important reason for participation on the part of juveniles.

3. The vast majority of youngsters tested had experienced and do experience in one form or another in their daily lives some degree of oppression. This was, on the basis of our questionnaire and interview studies, the most significant common denominator unifying all of the observed youngsters. A converse notion, i.e., the wish to

obtain self-respect and with it respect by others, seems, in our opinion, a dominant striving on the part of the black youngster.

4. Interviews with a randomly selected group of ten youngsters who were seen in their family homes along with a parental figure corroborated what the psychological test data tend to show; namely, that the participating youngsters are, generally speaking, normal adolescents who seem to have attained a higher level of psychological maturation and social adjustment than the average youngster whom we see in the Youth Home by reason of his delinquency. This finding is especially salient, and should be particularly emphasized as there is a prevailing but erroneous impression that participation in riot activity is synonymous with psychopathology.

5. A re-evaluation of the logistic information tends to substantiate our idea that juveniles avoided the Twelfth Street area. It is our impression that youngsters tended to be excluded from the illicit activity which was known to have been prevalent in the Twelfth Street area prior to the riot.

6. The mothers of the arrested youngsters revealed a most interesting group characteristic. It seemed that they went to lengths to warn their sons to avoid participation in the disturbance. In so doing, they frequently produced the opposite effect, namely to stimulate an irresistible wish on the youngster's part to see and partake of the action. This represents not so much a tactical error on the part of the mothers as, in our opinion, an unconscious wish

for their sons to be involved in what most feel to have been an historic revolutionary uprising.

Two contradictory attitudes on the part of the families studied were always observed: A moralistic reaction toward violence contrasted with the conviction that in the case of the Detroit riots the violence was justified and appropriate. The net effect on the children was that none of them was vilified or otherwise thought ill of within the family because of their participation in the riot.

7. We feel that there are major social and psychological changes occurring within the black community which are related to the following changes within the American culture:

  a. A resolution in the contradiction between role expectations for black and white youngsters, especially boys. This refers to the fact that aggressiveness and assertiveness, highly prized traits in the white culture, have been societally squelched in the black youngster in the past. The capacity to participate in rioting may reflect an improving sense of masculine role identification on the part of the black youngster. This is substantiated in various ways, particularly in the attitudinal survey and psychological tests which revealed evidence of a more positive masculinity in the arrested youngsters as compared to mine-run delinquent youngsters with whom we have come in contact in the past.

  b. We believe that the rising expectations theory is

applicable to riot participation in that we feel that the improvements in the Civil Rights field of the past decade have heightened the recognition of oppression on the part of the black community, and have moreover contributed materially to its sense of an inner capacity for change.

c. The much-discussed Moynihan report depicted a highly matriarchal black society in America. What we have observed suggests a new dimension in the role of the mother, namely tacit and vicarious use of her son to express her own abiding resentment of the oppressive conditions under which the black community lives.

8. Comparison of the ages of the arrested youngsters with their listed school grade suggests that the average arrestee was about one year behind in school. We suspect that this is not incompatible with the general population under discussion. It may reflect the acknowledged deficiencies in the education of black children.

9. None of the youngsters whom we studied were known to have been involved in arson or sniping. Our comments as to the normality and appropriateness of riot participation, therefore, do not include involvement in these offenses.

Appendix II:
Youth Home population

This exhibit shows the actual day the juveniles were released and not the day they were ordered released. The Referees ordered some juveniles released on personal bond of parents and then their parents did not show up for them for a day or two. Phone calls were placed and letters mailed to parents to come and get their sons. Some of these parents were themselves in jail for looting. What does a Judge do with a juvenile, caught looting with his parents, who has no previous Court record?

The maximum population of boys in the Youth Home reached 681. The rated population is 160. It will be noted that 355 were admitted on Monday and only 59 on Tuesday. It would appear that parents curtailed their children in their homes after the first two days of the riot even though the riot by the adults continued on a full scale.

Since the turn of the century, Youth Home personnel have kept their statistics for admittance from 8 A.M. on one day to 8 A.M. the following day, so the big drop in juveniles brought to the Youth Home did not occur until sometime between midnight on Monday and 8 A.M. on Tuesday. The reason for keeping statistics in this manner is lost in antiquity. Judge Lincoln has been on the bench seven years and was not aware of it until he challenged the Tuesday figure of 59 admittances as obviously incorrect. He then learned for the first time in seven years how statistics were actually compiled.

It should be noted that there were 171 boys in the Youth Home at the time the riot began. Most of these stayed in the Youth Home during the riot. The maximum number of those engaged in the riot continued in the Youth Home at its peak load was approximately 500, and the balance of the 681 were there prior to the riot.

One boy who was in the Youth Home for car theft prior to the riot was released at a Preliminary Hearing during the riot, and was arrested within twenty-four hours for looting. He was returned to the Youth Home a second time and stayed.

There is nothing in this chart that reflects the normal operation of the Wayne County Youth Home. It was built for 160 boys and 60 girls. There are usually well over 200 boys and about 90 girls in the Youth Home. However, two months out of the year the Youth Home population drops —July and August. This might be accounted for by the fact that upwards of several hundred thousand juveniles leave Wayne County on vacation. This is particularly true on weekends. Some of them get into trouble in other counties and undoubtedly the delinquency rates go up in the summer-resort areas in Michigan. Thus, there were only 171 boys in the Youth Home (11 over capacity) when the riot started. After the riot, many police were tied up on matters relating to adult cases. Besides, the rioters needed a rest. Whatever the reasons the Intake remained low for some time after the riot. This chart shows the situation immediately before, during, and after the riot.

YOUTH HOME POPULATION
BOYS ADMITTED AND RELEASED AND TOTAL

		ADMITTED	RELEASED	TOTAL
7/16/67		14	18	158
7/17		17	24	151
7/18		25	22	154
7/19		28	18	164
7/20		17	22	159
7/21		29	20	168
7/22		21	18	171
7/23	Sunday	161	5	327
7/24	Monday	355	10	672
7/25	Tuesday	59	50	681
7/26	Wednesday	35	37	679
7/27	Thursday	22	143	558
7/28	Friday	8	150	416
7/29	Saturday	13	134	295
7/30	Sunday	11	31	275
7/31	Monday	12	54	233
8/1		18	42	209
8/2		17	51	175
8/3		13	24	164
8/4		29	36	157
8/5		19	22	154
8/6		15	0	169

Appendix III:
Arrests of adults and
juveniles by Detroit police

This is a report of the Detroit Police Department. It does not include the juveniles, arrested in cities surrounding Detroit, who were brought to the Youth Home during the riot. The Detroit figures check out well with Youth Home statistics.

It should be remembered that this was an adult riot, not a juvenile riot.

REPORT OF DETROIT POLICE DEPARTMENT
Age, Race, and Sex of persons apprehended during
the civil disorder—July 23 through July 31 inclusive

AGE	WHITE MALE	FE-MALE	TOTAL	NEGRO MALE	FE-MALE	TOTAL	TOTAL OF BOTH
10	1	–	1	10	3	13	14
11	–	–	–	16	7	23	23
12	1	1	2	26	5	31	33
13	2	–	2	48	9	57	59
14	3	1	4	95	17	112	116
15	11	–	11	151	18	169	180
16	22	1	23	236	19	255	278
Total Juveniles	40	3	43	582	78	660	703

AGE	WHITE MALE	FE- MALE	TOTAL	NEGRO MALE	FE- MALE	TOTAL	TOTAL OF BOTH
17	25	7	32	207	46	253	285
18	20	9	29	210	49	259	288
19	16	8	24	212	39	251	275
20	63	12	75	264	43	307	382
21	29	3	32	258	35	294	326
22	23	4	27	243	26	270	297
23	29	–	29	264	31	295	324
24	35	1	36	249	38	287	323
25	24	3	27	211	30	241	268
26	12	1	13	183	24	208	221
27	33	–	33	293	23	316	349
28	34	–	34	270	16	286	320
29	49	2	51	247	14	261	312
30	9	–	9	129	18	148	157
31	11	–	11	108	18	128	139
32	13	–	13	97	19	116	129
33	14	2	16	109	12	121	137
34	5	–	5	96	13	109	114
35	6	1	7	88	14	102	109
36	10	–	10	82	15	97	107
37	6	1	7	93	17	110	117
38	6	–	6	78	15	93	99
39	9	1	10	67	11	78	88
40	5	–	5	72	14	86	91
41	5	–	5	60	8	68	73
42	7	1	8	65	10	75	83
43	4	–	4	41	10	51	55
44	6	–	6	49	3	52	58
45	1	–	1	43	3	46	47
46	2	1	3	40	10	50	53
47	3	–	3	39	4	43	46

AGE	WHITE MALE	FE-MALE	TOTAL	NEGRO MALE	FE-MALE	TOTAL	TOTAL OF BOTH
48	4	–	4	19	6	25	29
49	1	–	1	22	4	26	27
50	6	–	6	20	6	26	32
51	2	–	2	19	7	26	28
52	–	–	–	11	6	17	17
53	1	–	1	25	3	28	29
54	2	–	2	14	4	18	20
55	–	–	–	10	1	11	11
56	2	–	2	8	3	11	13
57	1	–	1	14	2	16	17
58	1	–	1	4	1	5	6
59	3	–	3	10	2	12	15
60 & Over	13	–	13	34	4	38	51
Total Adults	*550*	*57*	*607*	*4683*	*677*	*5360*	*5967*
GRAND TOTAL	*590*	*60*	*650*	*5265*	*755*	*6020*	*6670*

Appendix IV:
What happened to arrested juveniles after the riot was over?

Juvenile Court judges will be interested in the nature and extent of postriot problems that must be handled by the Court. (This part of the report was written in December 1967, approximately five months after the riot.)

Needless to say, extraordinary conditions prevailed, but let us review it from the beginning:

1. The police brought approximately 700 boys to the Youth Home for riot-related activities in a period of several days in July 1967. The Youth Home is designed to accommodate 160 boys.

2. These boys remained from one to four days in the Youth Home, sleeping on the floor in their own clothing, etc.

3. Either during or at the end of the riot, the greater portion were released either on bond or personal recognizance. Juveniles in Michigan are entitled to bond the same as adults.

4. The condition of Court personnel and also the police following the riot was similar to that of an army after a major battle. The police were also overburdened with problems relating to processing of adult cases.

5. There was some delay in determining how the bulk of the cases would be handled, for time was needed to evaluate each case. As it turned out, the Detroit police acted much faster than we anticipated. We also used a full time member of the Prosecutor's staff to help determine whether the police really had a legal case.

6. In the original screening process, the police dropped several hundred cases. The Detroit police alone reported they arrested 703 juvenile boys and girls. Added to this should be 70 or 80 arrested in other communities. Yet, a total of 461 delinquency petitions were requested by police. Approximately 300 cases were set aside by the police by their screening. This includes other police departments besides Detroit. This does not mean that the arrests were illegal. Probable cause existed in these cases; only a handful of juveniles was arrested illegally. But the police, together with William Cahalan, Prosecuting Attorney of Wayne County, and his Assistant Prosecutor, Edward S. Ferris, did a remarkable job in screening the cases themselves within a few weeks following the riot, eliminating those cases where there was a question of proving the case beyond a reasonable doubt or by a preponderance of the evidence. They did it under the most adverse of conditions for they were still beset with the major problem of the adult cases and of attempting to carry on normal police work.

However, if not beset with so many difficulties and given more time, it is probable that the police would have screened out many more cases that the Court eventually screened out.

7. Here are a few of the specific problems that confront the Court in determining whether or not to accept a delinquency petition:

    a. Can the witness be produced? Suppose the arrest was made by a National Guardsman or a paratrooper? The Lord only knows in what state or county he would be at the time of trial.

    b. If it were a misdemeanor arrest, such as violation of curfew, did a Guardsman have a legal right to arrest? Martial law was not declared, only an emergency proclaimed by the Governor. What right has a National Guardsman to arrest for a misdemeanor unless he is assisting a police officer?

    c. How can it be proved that the goods in the juvenile's possession were stolen? *Example:* the boy states at the Preliminary Hearing in the Youth Home, while the riot is in full bloom, that he was on Twelfth Street during the first day of the riot. Many adults were going into stores with the police standing by watching them, but doing nothing, so he went into the store and got some loot and took it home. The following day, he says he was in another store and got some loot, and while walking home with it the police apprehended him and brought him to the Youth Home.

      Of course, none of these statements is admissible, for they were made at a Preliminary Hearing when, for one reason or another, the parents were not present. A juvenile cannot waive his constitutional rights. He is put on $1,000 personal recognizance and the parents pick him up after the riot is drawing to a close. Many used the Court as baby-sitters during the riot. Where do we go from here? Even if the police and Prosecutor want to make a case, an attorney needs only to tell the boy to remain silent. Several hundred millions of dollars worth of merchandise was looted in Detroit. How can it be proven that any article of goods was stolen unless someone was caught in a store stealing it? In fact, many said they picked up articles on the sidewalk. Loot was everywhere. The problem is to prove that the merchandise was in fact stolen merchandise and that the defendant is, in fact, the one who took it.

8. What about cases where boys were charged with possession of flammable material (gas bottles with wicks found in trunks of automobiles)?

In these cases, an adult was invariably driving and there would be several in the car. Presumably it would be the adult in possession and a conviction might well be sustained against the adult. It is next to impossible to sustain a delinquency petition against the juvenile under such circumstances. There were approximately a dozen such cases where it was absolutely impossible to make a case against the juvenile, for it would be presumed that the adult was in possession. Invariably, the boy denied even knowing that the material was in the trunk.

9. The police and National Guard could not give the attention to individual cases during the riot they give in normal times.

Example: One boy threw a Coke bottle against a building and a citizen told either police or National Guard that he had seen the boy try to burn the building. The police arrested the boy in his home. Upon questioning the witness, the Prosecutor determined that there was no evidence at all of gasoline being in the bottle. No wick was found. The lad had just thrown an empty Coke bottle against the building as he walked by, as boys are apt to do. No case! The riot was a good time to pay off some old scores, and there is no doubt that this boy had harassed the complainant in the past; the boy was no angel and had a record.

10. After the police had screened out upwards of 300 cases themselves, it was necessary for the Court to do a very careful screening. The Wayne County Juvenile Court only had one Assistant Prosecutor to help with this job. He was of great assistance, but he could have used half a dozen Assistant Prosecutors to great advantage. The work was so voluminous that considerable personnel had to be assigned to it, and the bulk of the work had to be done by Court personnel. The determination of whether or not there is evidence enough to take a case to Court is more properly a function of the Prosecutor. Everyone did the best he could with the staff available.

11. What about the boys against whom cases can be made and the Court must decide whether or not to accept a petition?

   a. In ordinance violations, such as violation of the Governor's curfew, if the boy has already been in the Youth Home during the riot: Unless he was a probation violator from the Court or a parole violator from a State Training School, these cases were discarded, except for the fact that after being released on recognizance most of the boys were called in by the Court Clinic. No official petition would be taken in such a case.

b. It is hard to get figures to square exactly. A memo from the After-Care Unit of the State Training Schools states that nineteen parole violators were returned to them by the Court. The Intake Department of the Court reports only twelve such cases. The State figure is correct. There was much confusion during the riot. I remember calling the After-Care Unit of the State and asking them to take every one of their wards as quickly as possible because of congestion in the Youth Home. They complied with this request and somewhere along the line our Intake failed to account for seven of the nineteen in their report.

c. There is no breakdown by Intake on cases that were denied for lack of admissible evidence, or because of the fact that there was no prior police contact, or because the particular circumstances may not have warranted a petition even if the case might be proved. These questions were all mixed up together in the statistics. Considering the pressure under which the Court worked and the resources at our command, it is impossible to present a clear picture.

d. The Intake Department of the Court reports as follows:

1. Referred to Boys' Probation for Action   54
2. Referred to Neglect   6
3. Referred to Foster Home   7
4. Referred to Investigation Department   18
   (pending petitions)
5. Referred to After-Care (they actually
   got 19)   12
6. Referred to Other Counties (Oakland
   County)   3
7. Petitions filed by Intake   54

TOTAL   154

All this means, boiled down, is that 154 boys out of 700 were either retained by Intake, or referred to some other unit of the Court or to some State agency for action.

In the Wayne County Juvenile Court, if the boy is already on probation, the Boys' Unit of the Court and not Intake handles the case. If the boy is in a foster home on a neglect petition, the case is referred to the Foster Home Unit, and so on.

As a practical matter, the resource most needed by the Court to handle the bulk of riot cases does not exist. The Youth Home is always crowded beyond capacity and there is no place to confine a boy for ten, twenty, thirty, or ninety days; such an institution is at least five years away in Wayne County. The simple fact is that Wayne County has not provided the Court with the facility necessary properly to dispose of perhaps 100 of these riot cases. We are in fact under a directive to cut back on the services because of fiscal problems in Wayne County.

Several months ago, I wrote that juveniles were involved in looting and curfew violations, etc., and not in burning or shooting. There is one very notable exception. Some months after the riot, the police arrested a boy for burning a furniture store during the riot. There was an eyewitness and the police were several months locating the boy, who did not live at home. The boy had previously been sent to Boys' Training School and Juvenile Court had exhausted its facilities for working with him. He is now seventeen years of age. He was waived and his trial is pending in Recorder's Court in Detroit. So far as I can determine, there were only two cases where substantial evidence was produced that a juvenile was involved in a burning. Looking back on the past five months, one point stands out: *the Court was in a much better position to handle riot problems than to handle postriot problems.*

During the riot, normal operation of the Court was suspended. No cases were heard other than Preliminary Hearings, and Referees worked long hours to see that all juveniles were given a Preliminary Hearing within twenty-four hours. The normal work of probation officers ceased and many were assigned to help Intake and Release in the Youth Home. All Youth Home attendants worked long hours, some around the clock. Some Court personnel stayed at the Court or Youth Home around the clock (including the Judge). The National Guard, the paratroopers, and Deputy Sheriffs furnished additional manpower to operate the Youth Home. *One way or another, the resources were available and organized so that the riot problems were handled capably and efficiently.*

When the riot was over, the borrowed help left. Probation officers and similar personnel temporarily relieved of their overloaded caseloads, and the Referees relieved of their overcrowded dockets, returned to their normal routines. The Youth Home was soon back to normal operation, which means operating at overcapacity with attendants complaining about overcrowded wards. Then, of course, came the directive to make mandatory savings at both the Court and the Youth Home because of fiscal problems that confront Wayne County.

With too few resources to handle normal operation, the postriot problems are anything but welcome. *It is a paradox that in the nearly eight years I have been on the bench, the only time I have had proper resources to handle the task at hand was during the week of the July riot.*

Appendix V:
Directive of riot procedure issued on July 29, 1966, a year before the riot

COMMENTS

1. The police and sheriff were unable to release enough manpower to handle the crisis at the Youth Home. Prior arrangements should have been made to get the National Guard to the Youth Home early in the riot.

2. There is no need to clear out wards for juveniles picked up in the riot. Put them in with the delinquents who were there before the riot.

3. Ten juveniles were conveyed to jail from the Youth Home because they attempted to instigate a breakout prior to the arrival of the National Guard.

4. The decision to keep the overflow in the gymnasiums and auditorium made it possible to keep the juveniles, the records, and the hearing officer in one building. This was a most important decision.

5. Prior to the riot we were unable to foresee the exact way in which procedures had to be modified to process juveniles.

Basic problems had been discussed with supervisors in the Court, the Youth Home, the Sheriff, and the Police Commissioner a year before the riot (1966) and a written riot procedure issued by Judge Lincoln. The fact that this work had been done prior to the riot resulted in a more efficient handling of the problems when the riot came in 1967. Now that the Court has had the experience of handling the problems created by a riot, it has been possible to write a much better riot procedure and make it available to other Juvenile Court judges. This is one of the chief objectives of the first portion of this riot report.

PROBATE COURT

JUVENILE DIVISION

WAYNE COUNTY, MICHIGAN

Detroit 7, Mich.

(Effective July 1966)

MEMORANDUM CONCERNING PROCEDURE TO BE USED IN EVENT OF SUDDEN INCREASE IN POPULATION OF WAYNE COUNTY YOUTH HOME DUE TO CIVIC DISORDER.

1. EARLY NOTICE OF TROUBLE WILL BE GIVEN BY:
   A. Intake Personnel of Court.
   B. The Police Department, particularly the Youth Bureau and the 13th Precinct.
2. NOTICE WILL BE GIVEN TO ONE OR MORE OF THE FOLLOWING:
   A. Judge James H. Lincoln
   B. John Kurland, Register of the Wayne County Juvenile Court
   C. Harlan Ringelberg, Director of Intake, Wayne County Juvenile Court

   D. Anthony B. Caffrey, Director of the Wayne County
      Youth Home
   E. Intake
      (The first person who receives a call from Intake or
      the Police concerning this matter has the obligation
      of notifying the other three, if in his judgment cir-
      cumstances warrant.)
3. COMMISSIONER GIRARDIN HAS DESIGNATED
   THE YOUTH BUREAU AND THE 13TH PRECINCT
   AS CONTACT POINTS FOR THE COURT. THE
   SHERIFF'S OFFICE IS AVAILABLE FOR ASSIST-
   ANCE.

Either the sheriff or the Detroit Police will be available for
the following:
   A. To furnish the services of 5–10 policemen and/or
      deputies upon request to be detailed to the Youth
      Home immediately.
   B. To assist in problems of transportation to Jail—
      Receiving Hospital.
   C. To, in general, cooperate in working out problems
      with the Court so that speedy and necessary action
      may be taken.
Both the Sheriff's Office and the Detroit Police Depart-
ment are available for assistance.

Obviously, the Detroit Police Commissioner will determine the extent and amount of assistance that can be
given on request of the Court. However, it will expedite
matters by having the Youth Bureau and the 13th Precinct understand that they can give limited assistance

immediately upon request without referring the matter to higher authority.

OPERATION OF YOUTH HOME DURING EMERGENCY

A. *One unit will be vacated for the new arrivals.*

B. It will be the policy not to mix those brought to the Youth Home for civic disorders with other juveniles already in the Youth Home. Obviously, it may not be possible to implement this policy by 100% separation.

C. The juveniles in the ward that is vacated will be placed in other wards.

D. The usual admission procedures will continue so far as practical. Juveniles retain constitutional and legal rights during civic disorders. There will be preliminary hearings the day following admittance to see if each juvenile should be held until his regular hearing.

E. No juvenile will be conveyed to the County Jail except on an order signed by the Judge.

F. *Should the vacated ward become overcrowded, additional space will be provided in the following manner:*

  1. Another ward will be vacated in the same manner as the first, provided this is possible.

  2. Some juveniles may be conveyed to the County Jail, depending on circumstances.

  3. If necessary the gymnasium of the Youth Home will be used as a place of detention.

It will be the policy to use Youth Home and Court personnel to handle our own problems. Requests to Police agencies will be kept at a minimum. Whenever a juvenile may be legally held and his release would tend to promote further civic disorder, it will be the policy to detain him in the Youth Home regardless of the extraordinary means that must be taken to provide space and facilities.

James H. Lincoln
Judge of Probate
Juvenile Division

JHL:s
EFFECTIVE: July 29, 1966

Appendix VI:
Activities in communities
near Detroit during the riot

1. Thirteen communities in Wayne County reported no arrests of juveniles during the riot.

2. The police in five communities in Wayne County arrested a total of fifty-one juveniles during the riot, but conveyed *none* of them to the Youth Home, which they knew to be overcrowded to a point where they did not try to get them admitted. Most of these violations were breaking and enterings, car thefts, and the general variety of offenses which ordinarily come to our attention.

3. The police in Highland Park, which is located within the geographical confines of Detroit, arrested twenty-eight juveniles and brought sixteen of them to the Youth Home. Most of them were apprehended for violating the Governor's curfew.

4. The police in Grosse Pointe Woods brought two boys to the Youth Home for violating the Governor's curfew.

5. The police in Hamtramck, which is within the geographical confines of Detroit, brought ten juveniles to the Youth Home for violation of curfew. However, there was no riot in Hamtramck. Most of those arrested in Hamtramck were not residents of Hamtramck.

Only a few juveniles from other communities were arrested in Detroit during the riot. Highland Park had the greatest number; twenty-one juveniles from Highland Park were arrested by Detroit police.

For the most part, it was a Detroit riot, with nothing more than the usual activities in nearby cities. Most of the Detroit juveniles arrested in the riot were within fairly easy walking distance from home.

Appendix VII:
Example of police admittance sheet to Youth Home

ADMISSION RECORD

WAYNE COUNTY YOUTH HOME................ ☒

D. J. HEALY CHILDREN'S CENTER............... ☐

(Check One)

ADMITTED
Date July 24, 1967
Time 2:30 PM
By Allen
Locker No. 482
Unit No. Boys Gym
Property Yes
Money $6.86

Name...........TURNER, Melvin.. Age.................

Living With...Mother......................xxxx Kercheval.......................
                                                    ADDRESS

Father ....George Turner.........................Unknown.....................
                                                    ADDRESS

Mother .....Thelma Turner..........xxxx Kercheval.........................
                                                    ADDRESS

Arrested by..Patr. Thomas Herndon...Precinct....1........

Arrested at..3143 Woodward...........................Date..7-24-67.....Time..........1:20 PM......

Child Resides in Precinct..........1........................Arrested in Precinct................1.............

Date of Birth...4-1-51............Religion..Protestant.......School.Northeastern.......Grade....10........

White.................Negro.....X.........Other................. Employment.....Stockboy.............................

Charge.....B.&.E,.B.P. -. Looting....................... Previous Admissions....None......................

.... On Probation to..........No.......................

Sent in by..Larry Haas........................... Parents Notified by......Larry Haas...................
          Rank..Patr........ Pct.1.YB.......... Rank...Patr........ Pct......1.YB......

REASONS FOR DETENTION:

Officers apprehended Defendant at above time and place in loan shop. Defendant, who was in the shop had a 9 transistor Shaw portable radio in his possession, radio on Evid Tag 685233. Defendant was with 4 others at scene, during civil disturbance.

7/27/67 - 10:15 AM.
OK to release to mother
on $1,000. Per, recog —

7/25/67
Detain in Detention
Home. to Court for
determination of status
Bond $1500
Continued for appearance

(Registering Officer Leave Blank)

Police Officer.. Disposition......................................

File No........................Serial No........................

WAYNE COUNTY JUVENILE COURT

1025 E. FOREST AVENUE

DETROIT, MICHIGAN 48207

TO ALL LAW ENFORCEMENT OFFICERS:

THE BEARER OF THIS LETTER_____
IS AN EMPLOYEE OF THE WAYNE COUNTY JU-
VENILE COURT AND YOUTH HOME, AND IT IS
ESSENTIAL THAT HE BE PERMITTED TO TRAVEL
FROM HOME AND TO THE YOUTH HOME AND
BACK DURING THIS EMERGENCY. PLEASE PER-
MIT HIM TO PASS.

JAMES H. LINCOLN

JUDGE OF PROBATE

WAYNE COUNTY JUVENILE COURT

DETROIT, MICHIGAN

JHL:vbu

–July 24, 1967

[This letter of identification was given to approximately
200 Youth Home and Court employees during the riot.
One probation officer was picked up for violation of
curfew and spent thirty hours in a police precinct jail
until located and released by direct intervention of
Judge Lincoln. With this one exception, the letter
served its purpose.]

WAYNE COUNTY JUVENILE COURT
RECOGNIZANCE BOND TO APPEAR IN THE JUVENILE COURT

Re:

Born on:

We do freely acknowledge ourselves to be indebted to the people of the State of Michigan in the sum of One Thousand Dollars ($1,000.00) for the use of the said people if the following is violated.

The conditions of this recognizance are such that if the above shall appear in the Wayne County Juvenile Court when requested by the Court and shall not depart without leave or until discharged by due course of the law, then this recognizance shall be void, otherwise it is to remain in full force and effect.

_____

Signature of boy

_____

Parent

Dated_____

_____

Home address

Witnessed by:_____

Appendix X:
Agreement between state and county
whereby the state agrees to furnish
space for detained juveniles (July 26, 1967)

GEORGE ROMNEY, GOVERNOR
DEPARTMENT OF SOCIAL SERVICES
LEWIS CASS BUILDING, LANSING, MICHIGAN 48913
R. BERNARD HOUSTON, DIRECTOR

July 26, 1967

Honorable James H. Lincoln
Judge of Probate
Juvenile Division
1065 East Forest Avenue
Detroit, Michigan 48207

Dear Judge Lincoln:

This is in response to your telegram to Governor Romney
whereby you have requested assistance to detain the large
number of juveniles arrested as a result of the Civil dis-

turbance in Detroit. We have considered your request for space at the Boys Training School and have been advised by the Attorney General's office that the Department of Social Services has authority under P.A. 280 of 1939, as amended, to establish and operate regional detention facilities. Accordingly, we are proposing to establish Housing Unit C at the W. J. Maxey School at Whitmore Lake as a Wayne County detention facility annex. This facility will be so used for the period of time necessary to expedite the processing of court cases for those who have been arrested for law violations which have occurred during this current disturbance. It is expected that this emergency will terminate on or before 12-1-67. The following conditions are mutually agreed upon by the Wayne County Juvenile Court and the Department of Social Services:

1. That a legal order of detention will be issued on all such children under the age of 17 under the provisions of sections 14, 15 and 16 of Chapter 12a of Act 288 of the Public Acts of 1939, as amended, being sections 712a.14 and 712a.16 of the Compiled Laws of 1948.
2. The Wayne County Juvenile Court agrees to assign staff to this unit for the purpose of scheduling and communicating with the court regarding the establishment of hearing dates; and will assume responsibility for handling parent and legal counsel contacts.
3. The Wayne County Juvenile Court will assume responsibility for all conveyances to and from this temporary detention facility.
4. The Department of Social Services will provide all

custodial services including food, shelter, medical, clothing, etc. The Wayne County Division of the Probate Court shall be liable for 50% of the cost of care on a per diem basis.

5. The Department of Social Services agrees to provide staff to operate (which will require outside assistance) and will establish policy and regulations necessary to provide appropriate care and to maintain proper discipline.

6. The Department of Social Services reserves the right to return to the Juvenile Court any child who is too emotionally unstable or is incorrigible to the point where he cannot be maintained in this specific unit. It should be noted that Unit C is a medium security facility.

7. The Department of Social Services reserves the right to restrict the number of boys which can be housed in this facility at any one time. Insofar as possible, however, the department will endeavor to make maximum use of this facility (maximum capacity is 150 boys) for the purpose as stated in this proposal.

The above agreement is predicated upon the ability of the Department of Social Services to obtain adequate staff and funds to carry out the conditions of this agreement.

If you find the above proposal acceptable, please sign one copy of the attached and return to my office.

Yours very truly,

R. Bernard Houston

Director

I hereby accept the provisions of this proposal and agree to the conditions contained therein.

James H. Lincoln

James H. Lincoln

Wayne County Juvenile Court

c: Governor George Romney

Frank Kelley, Attorney General

[*Note:* It proved unnecessary to use these arrangements, which were worked out on the telephone during the riot. The National Guard would have provided the staff needs.]

Appendix XI:
Letter from Department of Social Services
(November 6, 1967)

STATE OF MICHIGAN

GEORGE ROMNEY, GOVERNOR
DEPARTMENT OF SOCIAL SERVICES
LEWIS CASS BUILDING, LANSING, MICHIGAN 48913
R. BERNARD HOUSTON, DIRECTOR
November 6, 1967

Honorable James H. Lincoln
Judge of Probate
Wayne County Juvenile Division
1025 East Forrest
Detroit, Michigan 48207

Dear Judge Lincoln:

Much has been said and written as an aftermath of the July 1967 civil disturbance in Detroit regarding law enforcement and court actions. We are all aware that much of this dialogue has been in the form of criticisms for the way the system operated. No mention to our knowledge has been made, however, for the competent, effective operation of the Juvenile Court and Youth Home programs during this critical period. Hartford Smith, Intake and Screening Unit Supervisor, State Department of Social Services, and I want to take this opportunity to let you and others know of our feelings on this matter.

While close enough to intimately know the magnitude of the problem, yet far enough removed to remain reasonably objective, it is our considered judgment that you and your staff performed a superior service in handling the 700 plus youngsters who were brought into the Youth Home for care and disposition during the crisis. We are most impressed with the pre-arranged plan which was ready for implementation to meet such an emergency and with the priority care exercised to insure the protection of legal due process and individual rights of the youngsters involved.

You and the staff who labored long and hard during this situation are to be commended for the philosophy employed, the emergency procedures implemented, for the custodial care rendered under most trying conditions, and for the judicious disposition of cases both at and beyond the preliminary hearings.

Perhaps it can be construed as a compliment in a negative sort of way that no public criticisms were directed at the Juvenile Court operation. In our opinion, however, this is an inadequate recognition of the strengths displayed and the services rendered by the Juvenile Court to the City of Detroit and, more importantly, to the youth of Detroit. We extend our sincere compliments on a job well done.

                    Yours truly
                        Hartford Smith
                    Hartford Smith, Supervisor
                    Wayne County Intake & Screening Unit
                    State Department of Social Services

                    Vergil M. Pinckney
                    Vergil M. Pinckney, Superintendent
                    Boys Training School

cc: Honorable Jerome Cavanaugh, Mayor
        City of Detroit
    R. Bernard Houston, Director
        State Department of Social Services
    Honorable Robert L. Drake,
        Deputy Court Administrator
        Michigan Supreme Court
    Honorable Glenn E. Jordon, President
        Michigan Probate Judges Association
    Mrs. Barbara Watt, Associate Director
        State Department of Social Services
        Bureau of Group Care Services
    Paul Conlan, Director
        Wayne County Department of Social Services

The Juvenile Court in Michigan began to function in the year 1907, when the State legislature of that year passed an act giving the Probate Court jurisdiction over delinquents and dependents. Michigan was one of the leaders among the states in establishing a separate tribunal for dealing with juvenile offenders. The first Juvenile Court in the United States was established in Cook County (Chicago), Illinois, in 1899.

When the 1908 constitution of the State of Michigan was adopted, the following section was incorporated:

> *Article VII, Section 13*
> In each county organized for judicial purposes, there shall be a Probate Court. The jurisdiction, powers and duties of such courts and of the judges thereof shall be prescribed by law, and they shall also have original jurisdiction in all cases of juvenile delinquents and dependents.

The constitution adopted in 1963, Article VI, Section 15 (last sentence) states: "They [the Probate Court] shall have original jurisdiction in all cases of juvenile delinquents and dependents, except as otherwise provided by law." This constitutional authority over delinquents and dependents means that no other court except the Probate Court can take any action in the matter of a child under the age of seventeen alleged to be delinquent or dependent.

For more than thirty-five years prior to the establishment of Juvenile Courts in Michigan, the State had recognized that delinquent and dependent children needed special care and treatment. Beginning in 1871 with the establishment of a State Public School for dependent children in Coldwater, Michigan, various laws were passed setting up new procedures in dealing with these two classes of children. In 1873 a State Agency System to deal with juvenile offenders was founded. The State Agent was a designated person, so named in each county, having authority to intercede in criminal cases involving juveniles. His function was to investigate cases, to supervise the juvenile in lieu of imprisonment, and to act as a parole officer. Laws were also passed separating the detention and trial of juvenile offenders from adult criminals.

The term "Juvenile Court" is descriptive and is merely used for convenience to designate the division of the Probate Court which deals with delinquents and dependents; it is not a separate court in and of itself. Its true designation should be the Juvenile Division of the Probate Court.

In accordance with the constitutional provision, there is a Probate Court in each county of the State. In all but a few of the counties there is but one Judge of Probate, who handles all of the work of the Court, such as the probating of wills, distribution of estates of deceased persons, commitment of mentally incompetent persons to institutions, adoptions, and cases involving dependent and neglected and delinquent children.

In Wayne County there are six Judges of Probate: Joseph A. Murphy, Thomas C. Murphy, Ernest C. Boehm, Ira G. Kaufman, Frank S. Szymanski, and James H. Lincoln. Due to the large volume of work in the Juvenile Division, Judge Lincoln has been designated to handle this branch of the Court and devotes his entire time to it, leaving the other work of the Probate Court to the remaining five judges. There are also five full-time Referees who assist Judge Lincoln in hearing cases. The 1967 budget provides for two additional full-time referees.

The philosophy and goals of the Juvenile Court is best stated in the first paragraph of the Juvenile Code:

> *712A.1 Juvenile Division of Probate Court, proceedings not criminal. Sec. 1.* While proceeding under this chapter, the Probate Court shall be termed the Juvenile Division of the Probate Court. Proceedings under this chapter shall not be deemed to be criminal proceedings.
>
> This chapter shall be liberally construed to the end that each child coming within the jurisdiction of the Court shall receive such care, guidance and control, preferably in his own home, as will be conducive to the child's welfare and the best interest of the State and that when such child is removed from the control of his parents, the Court shall secure for him care as nearly as possible equivalent to the care which should have been given to him by them.

Since its inception, the scope and functions of the Juvenile Court have been enlarged. The following paragraphs list some of the major services of the Wayne County Juvenile Court.

1. *Adoptions.* Petitions for the adoption of all minor children in Wayne County must be filed with and approved by this Court before the adoption becomes legal. The Court is interested in the background of the natural and adopting parents in order that the child may have a reasonable opportunity to grow up and enjoy a normal life.

2. *Dependent and Neglected Children.* The Court offers protection to children whose parents prove unfit to care for and supervise them. The children frequently are removed from the custody of their parents and placed at county expense in boarding homes through private child-caring agencies where they will receive proper care and supervision. The Court also operates a Court Foster Care Unit which supervises children who need specialized boarding homes and supervision.

When it is necessary to remove a child from the parents, the Judge makes a determination as to the parents' ability to pay support for the care of their children and enters a reimbursement order. A Collections Department enforces the order and parents are brought in for hearing when they are delinquent in their payments.

3. *Delinquent Children.* The Court handles the cases of children under the age of seventeen who are charged with a violation of law. The philosophy of the Court is that of reformation and correction. The procedure followed is that of trying to discover through good case-work prac-

tices what factors caused the child to become delinquent, and then work with the child, family, and community to correct that situation. Where possible, cases are adjusted without the necessity of official Court action.

4. *Concurrent Jurisdiction.* The Court has concurrent jurisdiction over youths seventeen up to the age of nineteen who may be generally classed as *incorrigible* or *disobedient* to the lawful commands of their parents. However, most of the cases of seventeen- or eighteen-year-olds coming to the attention of this Court are those where a more serious offense has been committed and could have been tried in criminal courts. Through the cooperation of the Prosecutor's Office, however, the charges are reduced and the case referred to this Court. The boy or girl is thereby often saved from a criminal record and a possible jail sentence. The Juvenile Court, at the discretion of the Judge, may sentence a youth in this age group for thirty days in the County Jail.

When the alleged delinquent child is fifteen or sixteen years of age, the Probate Judge may in serious felony cases, upon the request of the Prosecutor's Office, waive jurisdiction and permit the criminal courts to try the case. This would occur only in instances in which the Juvenile Court had exhausted all its resources for the rehabilitation of the defendant.

5. *Traffic and Ordinance Violators.* The Court handles the cases of children under seventeen years of age who receive ordinance, pedestrian, and traffic violation tickets. It is necessary for the child and at least one parent to be present at the informal traffic-violation hearing. While no fines or jail sentences are possible, attendance at the Police

Drivers' School may be required, or the youth's driver's license may be suspended. The Court attempts to make the youth aware of his responsibility as a driver and to encourage safe driving habits. In traffic violations he is also liable, the same as an adult, for the assessment of points against him which could cause deprivation of his driver's license.

6. *Branch Office.* The Juvenile Court has a Branch Office located in the western part of the county which services those communities in the area outside the boundaries of Detroit. This office handles all but dependent and neglect cases and delinquent recidivists who are returned to the Court for new offenses or other planning.

7. *Wayne County Clinic for Child Study.* The Juvenile Court, in addition to the abovementioned functions, operates a psychiatric child clinic, the Wayne County Clinic for Child Study. In the Clinic, the more difficult problems that come to the attention of the Court are given intensive study and treatment. The Clinic, with its trained staff, can give psychological and psychiatric examinations and tests. Upon completion of their study the Clinic can recommend commitment to state hospitals when deemed necessary. The Clinic can also obtain whatever medical and physical examinations are necessary for diagnosis and treatment.

8. *Youth Home and Shelter Home.* The Court also supervises the Youth Home, which is not primarily a reformatory or correctional institution. Its purpose is to furnish temporary lodging, overnight or longer, for delinquent boys and girls, for abandoned or neglected children, for out-of-town runaway boys and girls found in Wayne County, and for an occasional juvenile who is incarcerated

at the request of federal authorities. Any child held any length of time is necessarily in custody for the purpose of a court hearing or to effect a placement plan.

The D. J. Healy Shelter Home, located in Patton Park, for the most part houses the younger children. Most of these are dependent and neglected children who naturally should not be detained with delinquents.

The Juvenile Code provides: Detention, pending hearing, shall be limited to the following children:

A. Those whose home conditions make immediate removal necessary;

B. Those who have run away from home;

C. Those whose offenses are so serious that release would endanger public safety;

D. Those detained for observation, study, and treatment by qualified experts.

The Juvenile Court, Youth Home, and D. J. Healy Shelter Home has a staff of 426. Its budget is more than $7 million of which about $3 million is for the care of more than 3,000 children in foster homes and institutions. There is one probation officer to every 8,000 children of school age in Wayne County. The Court needs 100 per cent more probation officers and much more space for juveniles in the Youth Homes.

The present total population of Wayne County is estimated at 2,768,000. The Wayne County Juvenile Court serves 43 communities. Obviously, the Court is greatly handicapped in carrying out its functions by lack of facilities and insufficient number of personnel.

The Michigan statutes covering the Juvenile Courts can be found in the Compiled Laws of 1948, Chapter 712A, Sections 1 through 28, as amended.

WAYNE COUNTY

COMMUNITY	AREA SQUARE MILES	POPULATION				OCCUPIED DWELLING UNITS			
		APRIL 1, 1960	JULY 1, 1966	CHANGE NUMBER	%	APRIL 1, 1960	JULY 1, 1966	CHANGE NUMBER	%
Allen Park (6)	7.16	37,052	42,500	5,448	15	9,419	10,700	1,281	14
Belleville	.96	1,921	2,100	179	9	606	670	64	11
Brownstown Twp. (7)	28.12	7,257	8,300	1,043	14	1,937	2,140	203	10
Canton Twp.	36.12	5,313	5,900	587	11	1,434	1,610	176	12
Dearborn	24.47	112,007	114,800	2,793	2	33,898	34,750	852	3
Dearborn Hgts. (8)	12.07	64,096	78,200	14,104	22	16,935	20,800	3,865	23
Detroit	139.61	1,670,144	1,640,000	-30,144	-2	514,837	510,000	-4,837	-1
Ecorse	2.74	17,328	18,400	1,072	6	4,891	5,200	309	6
Flat Rock	1.57	4,696	4,800	104	2	1,188	1,200	12	1
Garden City	5.87	38,017	41,400	3,383	9	9,109	9,900	791	9
Gibraltar	4.35	2,196	3,330	1,134	52	647	980	333	51
Grosse Ile. Twp.	10.44	6,318	7,900	1,582	25	1,714	2,130	416	24
Grosse Pointe	1.32	6,631	6,950	319	5	2,217	2,250	33	1
Grosse Pt. Farms	3.19	12,172	12,800	628	5	3,574	3,700	126	4
Grosse Pt. Park	2.71	15,457	15,800	343	2	4,648	4,700	52	1
Grosse Pt. Shores	1.72	2,192	2,800	608	28	624	800	176	28
Grosse Pt. Woods	3.33	18,580	21,600	3,020	16	5,236	6,120	884	17
Hamtramck	2.09	34,137	31,700	-2,437	-7	10,767	9,950	-817	-8
Harper Woods	2.63	19,995	22,200	2,205	11	5,383	6,200	817	15
Highland Park	2.96	38,063	36,400	-1,663	-4	13,820	13,400	-420	-3

| POPULATION | | | | COMMUNITY | AREA SQUARE MILES | OCCUPIED DWELLING UNITS | | | |
APRIL 1, 1960	JULY 1, 1966	CHANGE NUMBER	%			APRIL 1, 1960	JULY 1, 1966	CHANGE NUMBER	%
6,884	7,700	816	12	Huron Twp.	35.86	1,749	1,950	201	11
36,119	41,400	5,281	15	Inkster (8)	6.28	8,604	9,870	1,266	15
53,933	57,800	3,867	7	Lincoln Park	5.93	14,621	15,700	1,079	7
66,702	98,000	31,298	47	Livonia	35.86	17,014	25,200	8,186	48
13,089	14,700	1,611	12	Melvindale	2.72	3,731	4,240	509	14
2,982	3,400	418	14	Northville (pt.)	1.13	1,001	1,150	149	15
7,673*	8,200*	527	7	Northville Twp.	16.70	903	1,100	197	22
8,766	10,900	2,134	24	Plymouth	2.23	2,723	3,400	677	25
8,364*	12,700*	4,336	52	Plymouth Twp.	15.92	2,009	3,270	1,261	63
71,276	75,000	3,724	5	Redford Twp.	11.25	18,165	19,100	935	5
18,147	18,800	653	4	River Rouge	2.80	5,283	5,470	187	4
7,237	9,800	2,563	35	Riverview	4.44	1,718	2,400	682	40
2,026	3,050	1,024	51	Rockwood	2.70	524	770	246	47
15,233	17,700	2,467	16	Romulus Twp.	36.04	3,892	4,540	648	17
29,404	32,100	2,696	9	Southgate	6.84	7,226	7,950	724	10
5,972	6,930	958	16	Sumpter Twp.	37.46	1,496	1,730	234	16
49,658	59,000	9,342	19	Taylor Twp.	23.63	12,613	15,050	2,437	19
18,439	21,500	3,061	17	Trenton	7.35	4,821	5,550	729	15
9,509	10,700	1,191	13	Van Buren Twp.	36.16	2,514	2,830	316	13
19,071	20,000	929	5	Wayne (9)	6.01	5,843	6,000	157	3
57,706*	75,000*	17,294	30	Westland (9) (10)	20.42	12,688	19,000	6,312	50
1,016	1,040	24	2	Woodhaven (7)	6.30	250	260	10	4
43,519	44,700	1,181	3	Wyandotte	5.54	12,396	12,770	374	3
2,666,297	2,768,000	101,703	4	TOTAL	623.00	784,668	816,500	31,832	4

Detroit, Michigan
November 10, 1967

Judge James Lincoln
1025 East Forest
Detroit, Michigan

Dear Sir:

I am a Foster Parent with the Children's Aid Society. I have been with Aid for fifteen (15) years.

The time has come that children require so much more and demand to dress like other children and not like "prisoners" as they call it. Some of the Foster Mothers having children have gotten together and formed a committee to talk it over to see what could be done to keep the children happy. We want them to grow up to be the men and women of tomorrow. We enjoy ourselves trying to do a good job with them in school, home and church.

In 15 years I have had 10 boys in my home as Foster children. Out of the 10, I kept two of them for 15 years. There was only one boy that I had any outside trouble with. I gave up my 2 boys that I had for 15 years to let them get a little experience away from me. At the time they were 17 and 18 years of age. The 18-year-old graduated in June and was put off the Aid. This boy was dropped without a job and placed back with grandparents that were proven unfit to rear them, yet they took him there and dropped him in this home. He stayed there for two weeks and came back to me in the night and told me that he could not stand that type of life and did not appreciate living in their home. He asked me if I would see that he got a job so my husband got him a job at the plant with him. We also helped him get a room. Today he is working, saving money to go to college. His brother is still in school plays football and basketball and expects to earn a scholarship to college, if he is allowed to finish, but he tells me that his worker says that they will not be able to keep him until he graduates because he will be 18 years old in December and will not graduate until he is 19. Is this fair to the child when they are unable to help themselves. This type of ultimatum fills a child with hate to feel that no one cares. Their father was a veteran and they never miss school or even had a bad record but that meant nothing. Do you think that children such as the ones described deserve a chance in life?

It seems that the Court could make some provisions for girls and boys, giving them at least a deserving chance. Turning them out in the world without a job is certainly not fair.

The Foster Mothers Club is really interested in these children's welfare, and we are trying to go all out for them. A committee was sent to talk to Mr. Dorin concerning this matter. The subject of giving the foster parents a raise was brought up, because of the cost of living has gone up and you know how long it has been since we have had an increase. We do not get adequate clothing either. Mr. Dorin's reply was: "Why don't you give up if you are not satisfied." He spoke as if he and possibly the Agency also were not interested. If the clothing supplied does not fit, it is necessary to wait until all clothing orders are filled before an exchange can be made. Often you do not get a replacement.

Mr. Dorin states that the Court allows $15.90 per child and if we want more, go with Juvenile Court.

The question is, "who will care for these children if we give them up. It is not the fault of the child to have to go from place to place with no one to care. We are interested in the children's welfare. Why is the foster mother not allowed to get the money for the clothing also. I think teenagers need to be allowed to try on their clothes. It is alright for the little children to be given a box but the teenagers resent it. Most of them will not even look at the things handed to them and if the foster parent wants to keep them happy, she must take them out and buy them something they want to wear.

Judge Lincoln, I think that you will understand what I mean, being a Juvenile Court Judge you of all people should have some insight about the teen age problems. We have too many boys and girls so disgusted with the life they live being pointed out by the clothing they wear. If a boy grows up fast and cannot wear a suit for two years, they can't get another one. I know this to be a fact. I tried and had to go out and buy my boys suits because they grew too fast. A boy under size 12 can't get a suit for dress. How can they go to church and take part in society if no one cares. Children should be allowed to fit their shoes and not have them issued out as if they are not human. These things make them grow up with hate in their heart, hate for everything you do. They are not to blame for being taken from their parents to go into a cold world of what they call "hate."

Please read this letter carefully, maybe I haven't worded it right but I have raised my own children and grandchildren and I find that you really have to keep up with the time. With the teenagers now I have been very close with my boys and they talk frank with me and I understand them. I am not tired as yet but I want to see children happy.

You know that children cannot be well cared for on the $1.51 we get per day. It is necessary to put in our money or the child is being neglected. Giving a child a home life they don't even get a box of candy at Christmas. What do you think the child that is not in a home that cares gets.

Please consider these things. We are not going to give them up, we want consideration for them, we want to know that someone cares. These children are our men and women of tomorrow. We want good men and women not "hate." With no change in things there is no future.

The Foster Mothers Committee is very concerned.

Respectfully,

(Mrs.) *Susie Mae Ghosson*
Acting Co-Chairman
Foster Mothers Club

PROBATE COURT

JUVENILE DIVISION

WAYNE COUNTY, MICHIGAN

1025 E. Forest Avenue
Detroit 7, Mich.

December 13, 1967

Mrs. Susie M. Ghosson
Acting Co-Chairman
Foster Mothers Club
Detroit, Michigan 48208

Dear Mrs. Ghosson:

I am well aware that many children in foster homes in Michigan are actually living at poverty level. As a matter of fact, the actual sum received by many foster parents for care of children places the children below the threshold of poverty level.

Here are some of the things I have done to try to improve the situation:

1. I constantly ask the Auditors and Board of Supervisors of Wayne County for more money for foster care for the 3,000 children who are Court wards. There is a 15 mill tax limitation on real property by the State Constitution for County government, schools and townships and thus, by operation of the State Constitution, the County government operates in the red. I can get only a limited amount of help from this source. They do the best they can.

2. If the State of Michigan would pay 50-50 matching funds to the county for foster care, it would be possible to raise the standard of foster care. The State pays some now, but far less than 50%.

Three years ago, I introduced a Resolution and it was adopted by the Michigan Probate and Juvenile Court Judges Association asking the State Legislature to adopt a 50-50 matching formula into law. We succeeded in getting the Bill through the Michigan House of Representatives, but it never got out of one of the Senate committees. In 1968, we will try to get a Bill that will provide 75-25 matching funds.

If we were to get this Bill enacted into law, it would give every County in Michigan a large sum of money to divide between boarding homes and also institutions. It would not solve the problem completely, but it would be a long step forward in providing adequate care for neglected children in Michigan. I have taken trips to Lansing, written letters, sent telegrams and done everything in my power to get this legislation adopted.

Your letter is somewhat critical of Mr. Doran, but the fact is that he can do nothing. Children's Aid Society has nearly 1500 children who are wards of this Court. He does the best that he can with the money that the taxpayers give him. He constantly asks for more money. There is simply nothing he can do unless the taxpayers pay more money for foster children. He must also take care of administrative expenses out of the funds given to Children's Aid Society for foster care.

The Court keeps 400 to 500 children in Court boarding homes and the balance of the 3000 Court wards are with private agencies. The Court only keeps the children that the agencies cannot handle because of medical problems, behavior problems, etc. This Court's boarding homes receive more money than some agencies pay. But, Court boarding homes are still greatly underpaid and I recently had a delegation of Court boarding home mothers visit me and they said the same things that you are saying about private agencies.

There are probably 100,000 children who are in boarding homes as Court wards on neglect petitions in this nation. From what I know of the situation, it is clear that a very substantial number of these children who were taken from their parents for neglect are actually living at poverty level or below poverty level in the homes in which the Courts have placed them.

It is unbelievable that this situation exists in the most affluent nation of the world.

I can only say that I am fully aware of the situation, and I will continue to do what I can to correct it.

Sincerely,

James H. Lincoln
Judge of Probate
Juvenile Division

JHL:P

Appendix XIV:
*Local tax problems—Why Juvenile Courts do
not have personnel and facilities to be effective*

Nearly every community has complex and difficult problems that cannot be solved without citizen understanding. The problem of getting resources for the Juvenile Court in Wayne County is probably no more complex or difficult than that in many other places. Perhaps a statement of the situation in Wayne County would lend some understanding to complex situations that exist in many places in the nation.

1. County government in Michigan has limited taxing power and its chief source of revenue is property tax.

2. There is a constitutional limitation of fifteen mills per thousand assessed valuation of property tax. This fifteen mills must be divided among townships, schools, library, and county government.

3. The only way to get beyond the fifteen mills is to go to the voters on a special vote, and this suggestion is not a vote-getter for any public official. In 1949, I was nominated for the Detroit Board of Education. Instead of talking about my own election, I spoke repeatedly for an increase millage for schools. The voters, in their wisdom, defeated me in my bid for election, but passed the millage.

4. A sizable percentage of the adult population have

children in schools and are directly affected. Also, there are thousands of teachers who help sell these millage proposals to the voters. But school millages are often defeated even with these strong forces operating. However, school districts often get an increased millage by a vote of the people. The better the schools and the more affluent the people in the district, the more likely the millage will be adopted. Thus, the gap in services between school districts becomes wider each passing year.

5. County government, unlike schools, is in a most unfavorable position to get increased millage. By a margin of a few thousand votes in a county of 2,800,000 it was possible to get one additional mill some years ago. The authorization will soon run out; it was good for only five years.

6. If there is not a renewal of authorization of the one mill by the voters in 1968 in Wayne County, then Juvenile Court services will be cut far below their present level.

7. It is possible in Michigan for voters permanently to vote a county to be an eighteen-mill county instead of a fifteen-mill county. If county government got 1.5 over the fifteen mills, and the school were given the authority to use the other 1.5, that would be a fifty-fifty split of the additional three mills. Some school districts would not use it, but nine out of ten would—and they need it.

This proposal would be in place of just asking the voters to renew the one mill for the county, which can never be good for more than five years and which is so inadequate that the Court would never expand facilities or services.

8. As for the additional 1.5 mills authorized for the schools, it should be pointed out that it is the poorer districts that have the hardest time getting a millage vote

passed. The only way the values of homes are going to be maintained over a period of time is for Detroit schools to match the services of other communities. This statement is equally true of Inkster and other school districts in Wayne County. The worse the situation, the less the chance of finding a solution.

People who can afford to pay any reasonable amount of taxes will not raise their children where they cannot get quality education. They move on to another community. The over-all ability to pay taxes in a community is tied in directly with the quality of the school system. There is no other way to insure a tax base and property values in Detroit or any other community without maintaining a school system of the highest order. This is true of the other forty-three communities in Wayne County and everywhere else in the nation. If schools throughout a region do not maintain some quality in educational advantages, the citizens with the greatest ability to pay will move to the communities in the region that offer the best educational advantages for their children. The people who move into the region from other parts of the state or nation will determine where they will live within the region by using the schools as the determining factor providing they have sufficient income and taxpaying ability. *If schools deteriorate, the taxpaying power of the community deteriorates; it is as simple as that.*

It is certain that the Board of Supervisors must do one of two things in the fall of 1968

1. Place a referendum on the ballot for the voters of Wayne County to vote to make Wayne County an eight-

een-mill county in place of a fifteen-mill county (1.5 of the addition to schools and 1.5 to the county); or

2. Place a referendum on the ballot for the voters of Wayne County to renew the *one mill* that is expiring. This solution is inadequate but would at least prevent severe cutbacks in services.

Regardless of which proposal appears on the ballot, a NO vote will have the effect of cutting the services at Juvenile Court and the Youth Home. This is not a small cut, but a drastic one. The police, the newspapers, and the people constantly complain about inadequate services at Juvenile Court. It is true, but the Court's resources are as thin as tissue paper and, only five months after the riot, there is a directive to cut services in order to meet a mandatory savings. In the end, the voters are going to have to decide what to do about it.

Crime and delinquency are perhaps the major issues of the 1968 elections. It makes no difference who is in office if the tools are not made available to do the job. The Wayne County Juvenile Court can never be effective with 100 probation officers. Half of them are on neglect and not delinquency cases. Fifty probation officers cannot supervise the delinquency problems of a county that has a population of approximately 2,800,000. The situation is simply absurd. Nor can the Court do an effective job with its present inadequate Youth Home and no short-term rehabilitative facility. Yet the orders are to cut services in 1968, and unless the voters take action there will be further drastic cuts in 1969.

There will be many bills before the State Legislature and ordinances before the cities for the purpose of crack-

ing down on crime and delinquency. All of them put together do not amount to anything unless Courts have the
facilities and personnel to do a much-needed and effective
job of law enforcement.

Before becoming a Judge, I served five and one-half
years on the Common Council of the City of Detroit and
on the County Board of Supervisors, and have voted on
County and City budgets six times. Unless county government is soundly financed, Juvenile Court facilities and
personnel will continue to be cut even below present inadequate levels.

The County Board of Supervisors will never give Juvenile Court the tools necessary to do the job as long as it
operates at a deficit. Unless action is taken, there will be
fewer services given by the Wayne County Juvenile Court
in 1969 than in 1968.

[Following is the text of remarks by Arjay Miller, President, Ford Motor Company, at a meeting of the National Industrial Conference Board, Waldorf Astoria Hotel, New York, New York, Thursday, November 30, 1967]

Human values in the computer age

One of the penalties of rapid technological change is its unsettling effect on large numbers of people who view it as a threat to their well-being and to the established order. This has been true, we are told, from the very beginnings of industrial history.

It is especially true, I believe, of that shining symbol of modern technology—the computer.

My remarks today are prompted by the feeling that, in our eagerness to exploit the new technology, we have been looking at the trees and failing to see the forest. In our adulation of the computer and other new devices and techniques, we have dwelt too much on the amazing technological capabilities of new electronic hardware and have done far too little to demonstrate its equally amazing potential for advancing human welfare.

As a result, we are witnessing what might be called a human backlash—a perfectly understandable anxiety as to what will become of the individual in a society that makes increasing use of highly sophisticated machines and large organizations to do its work. Mixed with human awe and admiration of the new technology is a vague, disquieting fear that, because of the computer, man has somehow lost position in this world—has become less important in the scheme of things.

The manifestations of this anxiety are not hard to find. Most of us, I'm sure, feel a strong bond of sympathy with the university student who carried a sign reading "I am a human being; do not fold, bend or mutilate."

And I'm sure most of us share some apprehension at the knowledge that computers make it easier for the government to move into more and more phases of our personal affairs. There is always the suspicion that George Orwell's *1984* might not, after all, be a piece of literary fantasy.

In the course of constructing urban freeways in various parts of the country, engineers have sometimes relied too much on computers and have failed to make proper allowance for such factors as beauty or esthetic value. In some cases, a technically correct freeway network has threatened to lessen unnecessarily the attractiveness of the communities it is meant to serve.

These examples could be multiplied, but I think the lesson is clear: if technological progress is to have real meaning and human significance, it must be made to serve man in ways that he can understand and appreciate. As John W. Gardner reminds us:

"The basic American commitment is not to affluence, not to power, not to all the marvelously cushioned comforts of a well-fed nation, but to the liberation of the human spirit, the release of human potential and the enhancement of individual dignity."

Part of our problem is a widespread misconception of the purpose and uses of the computer. Some observers see a future in which decisions will be made not by men, but by computers—or at best, by a handful of men who are in tune with computers. Some fear that the people who run things will be concerned only with problems that can be reduced to numbers, ignoring such fundamental but immeasurable values as individualism, freedom, and beauty.

This obviously must not be allowed to happen. Our task is to focus on man and his needs—not on technology itself.

The computer is only a tool—an electronic device that is completely subject to human will. It is essentially a tool for problem-solving. It can provide decision information that previously was too costly, took too long to process, or was literally beyond human capabilities to obtain.

But the choice of problems to be solved, the establishment of priorities, and the broad outlines of the attack on these problems are decisions for men, not for computers.

It is largely because of the computer that we are able to undertake the broad-scale approach to problem-solving called system analysis. Speaking very broadly, systems analysis is simply a way of looking at problems and deciding how best to attack them. First, we set forth the objectives we are trying to attain. Next, we set forth all the elements or factors that influence our ability to achieve those objectives. Then, with a full picture of alternatives and the likely consequences of each, we can choose the course of action that offers the best combination of benefits and costs.

This is one of the most valuable developments of our time. Traditional methods of problem-solving are just not equal to the complex problems we face. We are able, thanks to the computer, to take a "total" approach—to see all elements of a problem in proper perspective.

Used in this way, the computer is an aid to thinking— not a substitute for thinking. It extends brainpower in much the same way that machine tools extend muscle power.

As a matter of fact, one of the best things about the computer is that it forces us to think through our problems logically before we can even turn it on. In order to program a computer, we must have clearly in mind what it is we are trying to accomplish and the various means by which we can achieve our goals.

Thus far, the new technology—systems analysis, computers, and the rest—has been used mainly to serve private ends. It has been used also, of course, for military purposes and for space activities, but these uses are for the most part highly technical and far removed from the everyday experience of the average person. The tangible benefits that the average man has gained are primarily in the form of greater choice of products, higher quality, lower costs and prices, elimination of much heavy or repetitive work, and greater freedom to enjoy leisure-time activities.

Our success in meeting private needs and wants is a

matter of proud record. More people enjoy more material advantages than was thought possible even a generation ago. Economic man has been well served in our society.

But what about our social needs, both old and new?

In the wake of rapid technological and economic progress have come a wave of new social problems—urban decay, air and water pollution, highway safety, to name a few—that we must learn to deal with effectively. And even our fantastic economic gains of the past twenty years have failed to eliminate such perennial, deep-rooted problems as poverty, crime, ignorance, and chronic unemployment.

Until recently, it made little difference whether or not we recognized these problems because we felt powerless to solve them. When problems are that big and complicated, the tendency is to ignore them, hope that someone else will find solutions or simply throw up our hands and admit defeat.

Today our mood is different. Rapid progress in some aspects of life has led us to anticipate equally rapid progress in all aspects. As our standard of living rises, we are less willing to accept the prevalence of ugliness, dirt, congestion, and crime. As affluence grows and education spreads, poverty and ignorance are no longer tolerable. As our vision of the future expands, we find it difficult to reconcile ourselves to the fact that as many as one-sixth of our fellow citizens are not sharing adequately—or, in some cases, at all—in our progress to date.

Today, as a matter of fact, there is no longer any excuse for inaction or ineffective action. We have the resources to attack our social ills effectively. Science and technology are giving us the means both to analyze our problems and to point out solutions. It is no longer a question of whether or not we can meet our social needs, but whether we will make the necessary effort to apply our capabilities to social as well as private goals.

Systems analysis can be a powerful tool for the solution of social problems. It forces us to consider new possibilities, new opportunities, and new choices of many kinds. It enables us to discard old methods and old limitations on thought and action. In this sense, with more freedom of choice, we can be more human.

What is required first is that we as a people establish our national goals and our priorities. This must be a conscious and continuing effort on our part. In producing for private consumption, the setting of goals and priorities is no problem. Output is automatically determined by the marketplace as millions of individuals satisfy their own private needs and wants. In seeking to shift emphasis from private goods to "public goods," however, we must consider carefully what will do the most good for the most people.

This involves, among other things, a set of moral or ethical judgments—a philosophical re-examination of our scale of values. And as we make our choices through normal political processes, we must face the fact that, even in a society as affluent as ours, there are simply not enough resources to meet all of our needs at the same time.

Within the broad framework established by popular choice, we should be able to tackle specific problems in an organized way, breaking them down into manageable pieces and setting realistic timetables for corrective action. From there, we can look at our resources and match them against the cost-effectiveness of each of the alternate approaches available. Where there are trade-offs involved, we should be able to choose intelligently what we will sacrifice in one area in order to achieve another, more desirable goal. Only in this way can we arrive at some sensible understanding as to how much we can do, how best it can be done, at what speed, and at what cost.

As we develop new plans for social action, we should recognize the advantages of large-scale organizations in handling the large-scale tasks required of us. The massive problems and opportunities facing our society must be matched by massive resources working efficiently toward common goals.

Does all this mean that the individual will somehow be submerged or lost in the shuffle? Not at all. On the contrary, there will be greater need and scope for individual effort than ever before. Large organizations, by their very size and complexity, offer a wide opportunity for utilization of an incredibly broad range of talents. Far from reducing the individual to the least common denominator, the effective organization must take advantage of the fact that human talents are not homogeneous and interchangeable.

The premium, as always, will be on smarter and more creative people—men and women with broad, well-balanced knowledge and skills.

One of the special tasks of big organizations is to create an environment favorable for creative people. It is no accident that those organizations which place great emphasis on computers and systems analysis are usually also dedicated to what is known as "free-form organization"—

a concept in which people and ideas take precedence over traditional departmental or divisional patterns. Because these groups recognize that *change* is the overriding characteristic of our time, they seek to encourage innovation and constant self-renewal through giving the greatest possible rein to the creative talent of individual managers and employees.

Technology becomes an invaluable aid when it is linked to this spirit of innovation and new enterprise. It can give form and force to sound ideas for human betterment. In the same sense, to fail to make the fullest use of all the new tools and techniques at our command would be to limit unnecessarily our human response to human needs.

Let me illustrate my general theme by turning now to a specific area in which it has particular relevance. I am convinced that of all the social problems demanding attention today, the most basic is the elimination of poverty in this country. It is from poverty that many other social ills spring, and any successful effort to eliminate or greatly reduce this malignant growth could bring about dramatic improvement in the general health of our society.

The poverty problem is gigantic, by any measure, and it will not yield without enormous effort on our part. Although about 7½ million people are now covered by some form of welfare assistance, the government estimates that 30 million people do not have incomes sufficient to provide an adequate living standard. That's nearly one-sixth of our total population.

From all reports, the present welfare and manpower programs are making unsatisfactory progress—they are failing to reach many of those who need help most, and they have not sufficiently improved the welfare of others. Some of the poor now receive help from two or more programs, while others in desperate need receive nothing at all. It is increasingly evident that many of our welfare programs are inefficient and wasteful, offering no hope of breaking the poverty cycle.

I believe strongly that it is now time for us to take a "total approach" that would reach all of the poor and not just certain segments. What I have in mind would include both direct income assistance to those in need and measures to increase employment of the disadvantaged.

A satisfactory plan of income assistance should have these three essential provisions:

First, it would preserve incentives to those able to work to get jobs and to increase their earnings as rapidly as possible;

Second, it would be efficient in the sense of getting money only to those in need, without favoring some and ignoring others, and

Third, it would be relatively simple to administer.

In my opinion, the proposal that meets these requirements best is one called the "negative income tax." Under this plan, a family with zero income would receive a basic allowance related to the size and composition of the family unit. When a member of a family began to earn income, the basic allowance would automatically be reduced by an offsetting tax, but not by a corresponding amount.

Thus a family with a member at work would always be better off than a family without anyone at work, in contrast to present situations where every dollar increase in earned income is entirely offset by withdrawal of a dollar in welfare payments. Because the family's total income would always go up, there would be an incentive to work and to increase earnings. As the family moved up the income scale, of course, it would switch from receiving negative income tax payments to *paying* income taxes in the normal manner.

The negative income tax idea is worthy of thorough study and testing by the federal government to ascertain, for example, what combinations of basic allowances and offsetting taxes on earned income might be most workable and most acceptable to society at large.

Since this system would embrace all persons in need of help, it could replace a number of existing public-assistance programs. Thus the net cost would be less than the gross cost of the assistance payments under this program. States and localities, however, would be free to continue portions of existing programs in order to compensate for unusually high living costs in certain areas or to meet other special needs.

Let me repeat that adoption of a negative-income-tax plan should be only one part of a total program to reduce dependency. The basic long-run approach to helping disadvantaged people who are able to work must, of course, be to improve their capability for work and to increase job opportunities. This requires, first, education and training to overcome lack of qualifications; second, incentives for trainees to improve their qualifications for employment and advancement, and, third, reduction of other barriers to employment and advancement.

As we all know, lack of qualifications is not the only barrier to the disadvantaged who seek employment. Fortunately, the social and psychological barriers of prejudice and unfamiliarity are being overcome. But more rapid progress is needed. Employment tests, for example, should be re-examined to make sure they measure genuine employment potential and not merely cultural background. Tight limitations on entry into certain occupations should be eliminated.

If we are to plan effectively, we need to know a great deal more about the circumstances and disabilities of the poor and about the kinds of incentives and opportunities we must make available to them if they are to join the ranks of the self-sufficient. A systems analysis approach could give us a much better picture of these and other major factors, such as basic job requirements and the ability of these groups to respond to various methods of training. Until we see the problem in its totality and understand its many ramifications and its many subproblems, we cannot expect more than piecemeal efforts and piecemeal results.

I have talked about the problem of poverty at some length because I believe strongly that if we can eliminate poverty from our society, we will have relieved many other problems growing from it. And we can approach with more skill and more confidence the other social ills that stand in the way of our aspirations for a better life.

For the first time in all recorded history, we have a sound and practical basis for optimism about man's future. This might seem paradoxical at a time when the world appears to be in terrible shape, what with war, riots, increasing crime, and the rise of a host of new problems added to the old.

But the fact is that we increasingly recognize the need for a change in our attitudes and in our old ways of doing things. The riots in Watts, in Newark, and in Detroit have shocked us into the realization that we cannot afford to dally on the road to social progress. We know that we must dare to experiment, to innovate socially, and to take big steps.

We now have the power, if we can but learn to use it, to break the mold of social apathy, of resignation to age-old human ills, of continued tolerance of the wide cleavage between our aspirations and reality. We have skills and resources, human and mechanical, to achieve more than we can imagine. We must not fail to use them effectively.

We are only at the beginning of what could represent a quantum jump not only in man's relationship to his environment but in man's relationship to man. We have nothing to fear from technology. The real problem lies in our own uncertain grasp of the tremendous God-given powers within us.

If we can summon the will and the intelligence to use boldly and humanely the promising new tools in our possession, ours will be remembered not as the Computer Age or the Space Age or the Cybernetics Age—but as the Age of Man.

Appendix XVI:
The handling of adults during the riot

by William L. Cahalan
Prosecuting Attorney of Wayne County [1]

The problems confronting the Wayne County Prosecuting Attorney's Office last summer during the riot in the city of Detroit can be likened to those of the keeper of a water reservoir who is confronted with a sudden cataclysmic deluge. He can't stem the water because the dam will break, he can't open the sluice and inundate the valley below, and he must at all costs preserve the water because it is precious.

The magnitude of the problem can be seen in the following statistics: the capacity of the county jail was 1,260. The jail population on the day before the riot was 1,099. The Prosecutor's staff assigned to Recorder's Court, a statutory court having jurisdiction of felonies and misdemeanors committed within the city of Detroit, consisted of 35 attorneys who processed 7,360 felony cases and 20,782 misdemeanor cases in the entire preceding year in that Court. Suddenly, in a week's time, 7,223 people were ar-

[1] An article that appeared in Volume 3, Number 6, *The Prosecutor*, journal of the National District Attorneys Association.

rested and had to be processed in the normal manner—expeditiously, according to law, with complete regard for all due process and the constitutional rights of each defendant.

Despite the fact that the criminal justice process was being flooded with extraordinary numbers of law violators, valiant efforts were made by all concerned, from the policeman to the judge, to see to it that the full constitutional rights of each defendant were protected. That many of the legal amenities of normal times could not be maintained during the height of the chaos is undeniable; but, everything considered, I doubt that in the history of civil disorder a higher standard of concern for the rights of the defendant has ever prevailed. That this was done will stand as a monument to the professional competence and integrity of the members of the Prosecuting Attorney's staff, the Judges of the Recorder's Court, the court personnel and the members of the law-enforcement agencies, most of whom worked to the very verge of physical exhaustion during this period.

There are those who criticized. But criticism is hindsight and a luxury permitted only those not charged with responsibility. It must be realized that during the first days of the emergency no one knew what the true situation was. However, certain facts were clear. Law and order had broken down in wide sections of the city. The Detroit Police Department, despite heroic efforts, could not cope with the lawlessness. Hundreds of fires were set by arsonists in many parts of the city and were raging. Snipers were widely active. Fifty-six persons were shot by snipers and unknown persons; 167 police were injured, one fatally. Every piece of firefighting equipment in the city was in constant use and many surrounding communities sent all their firefighting equipment into the city to assist. Every fireman worked for days without thought of rest under extremely hazardous conditions. A total of 273 firemen were injured. Two died, one by sniper fire. Thousands and thousands of persons were looting stores of food, liquor, clothing, furniture, and firearms. Pawnshops throughout the city were especial targets for the guns to be found there. Most important, no one could be certain that the riot was not the result of an organized plan, nor that the entire city would not be burned to the ground. That this was a distinct possibility no one can gainsay; the magnitude of the destruction inflicted on the city is frightening evidence of that.

The problems and frustrations which beset those charged with the administration of justice during the height of the riot can best be delineated by considering them as they arose in connection with each step in the normal judicial process from arrest through and including arraignment on an Information (Indictment).

First, there was the problem of arrest. Feature to yourself a single police officer coming upon 50 persons—men, women and children—the latter following the example, if not the behest, of their elders—looting a supermarket. How does he arrest them? He gives a command. Some obey and some run, either with the loot or after dropping it. A handful of persons are arrested with their loot.

Although ony a fraction of all law violators were arrested during the rioting, that fraction amounted to a lot

of people. And each had to be booked at the police precinct station and a "write-up" made describing in detail
the circumstances of the commission of the crime and the
arrest.

An interesting aspect of police work at this point was
the use of photographs. The police knew that the individual police officer could not possibly remember all the persons whom he had arrested and the loot with which such
persons were apprehended and the circumstances of the
arrest when it came time to testify in court. In many precincts, therefore, the arresting officer and the accused
were photographed with a Polaroid camera side by side
with the loot piled on the floor before them. On the back
of the photo, particulars of name, location of arrest, etc.,
were noted. These photos were placed in the police file
folder of the case and were referred to by the arresting
officer just before his taking the witness stand for the
purpose of refreshing his recollection. They proved an
invaluable aid to the police officers.

After the write-up was completed, the officer in charge
of the case, a detective, then had to go to downtown Detroit to the office of the Prosecuting Attorney and present
the write-up to an assistant prosecuting attorney, who,
upon reading it, decided whether to make a recommendation to the magistrate to issue a warrant. Without such
recommendation, by statute, the magistrate had not the
authority to issue a warrant.

If the recommendation were issued, a formal complaint
and a warrant of arrest were typed. Here the first big bottleneck developed. There were just so many clerks available

who knew how to type a complaint and warrant, so a
backlog developed at this point while the girls labored
unceasingly to type the required documents.

In the meantime, the prisoners had been transported
downtown at the same time that the write-ups were
brought downtown. They had to be housed somewhere.
At this point, custody of the prisoners was not the legal
responsibility of the sheriff; it was the responsibility of
the Detroit police. Therefore, the prisoners were placed
in detention areas under their jurisdiction—that is, in
some one of the 13 detention cells in the court building,
on the ninth floor of Police Headquarters, and, when
space ran out, in buses parked alongside the court building and in an improvised area in the police garage—
there to await their arraignment. Those who were charged
with placing the prisoners in the detention areas did so
initially on an available space basis, without any particular order, so that when the complaint and warrant in a
particular case were ready the prisoner had to be searched
for throughout the various detention areas. Locating him
was time consuming and frustrating, especially since
many who were arrested had given false names and
others, to avoid arraignment, refused to answer to their
names. After the initial confusion, however, the police
began placing their prisoners systematically so that each
was easily located when needed.

The bulk of the recommendations made by the assistant
prosecutors who were detailed to this job were for looting
and for violation of the Governor's executive order which
imposed, *inter alia,* a curfew on the residents of the city.
Looting was charged as entering without breaking with

intent to commit larceny.[2] Of the total arrests which carried through to prosecution, 2,663, or 54.6 per cent, were for looting. The assistant prosecutors wisely decided that proof of an actual breaking was lacking in most of the cases, so that the proper charge was as stated since the prisoner had been caught within the store with a bundle of groceries or fifths of whiskey, or a television set.

The setting of bail on arraignment on the warrant was, of course, solely the function of the court. When it became clear on Sunday night that a full-scale riot was in process, I publicly announced that I was recommending a $10,000 bond on all those arrested for looting. The courts generally followed that recommendation, and some criticism ensued in the form of statements to the effect that the riot was extraneous to the individual consideration of bond and to the point that it was considered by some to be excessively high. I felt then, and I still feel, that the Court's response to my recommendation was justified.

Under Michigan law, the magistrate in setting bail may consider:

> . . . the seriousness of the offense charged, the previous criminal record of the defendant and the probability or improbability[3] of his appearing at the trial of the cause.

[2] "Any person who, without breaking, shall enter any dwelling, house, tent, office, shore, shop, warehouse, barn, granary, factory or other building, boat, ship, railroad car, or structure used or kept for public or private use, or any private apartment therein, with intent to commit a felony or any larcency therein, shall be guilty of a felony punishable by imprisonment in the state prison not more than 5 years, or fined not more than $2,500.00." Act 133, PA 1964; MSA 28.306.

[3] Comp. Law. '48 Sec. 765.6; MSA 28.893.

He may also consider surrounding circumstances. In *People* v. *McDonald*,[4] the Michigan Supreme Court quoted with approval Tiffany's Criminal Law (How. 4th ed.), 143:

> It (bail) should be determined from a regard to the nature of the alleged offense, its punishment, the standing, character, and property of the person charged, and *all the circumstances of the case*. [Emphasis added.]

And it is widely recognized that the court should keep in mind the good of the public in setting bail.

> In fixing the amount of bail, the good of the public as well as the rights of the person accused must be considered. *Braden* v. *Lady*, 276 SW2d 664, 8 CJS Bail Sec. 49, 135. The gist of the problem confronting a court in setting the amount of bail is to place the amount high enough reasonably to assure the presence of defendant when it is required, and at the same time to avoid a figure higher than that reasonably calculated to fulfill this purpose, and therefore excessive. In other words, in determining the amount of bail, the good of the public as well as the right of the accused should be kept in mind. 8 Am. Jur. 2d Sec. 70, p. 824.

The Court met its obligation forthrightly. Bail was set in all cases commensurate with the charges brought with due regard to the circumstances out of which the charge arose. Generally, the Court was guided by two important considerations. First, at the time of the arraignment of the prisoner on the warrant, his arrest record had not been located. This was so because there just wasn't time to

---

[4] 223 Mich. 98, 106.

search the records of the police identification bureau for previous arrests and convictions of the great numbers who were arrested, as will be more fully explained. Therefore, the magistrate had no way of knowing with whom he was dealing. Secondly, there was chaos and complete lawlessness in the streets in the areas where these prisoners had been arrested for criminal activity with police resources taxed to the fullest.

Surely, an individual riot case could not and should not have been abstracted from the social milieu in which it occurred; and the "circumstances" of the case are in part the socio-legal implications of the commission of that individual crime and thousands like it at the same time. Espionage in peacetime is not the heinous crime it is during perils of war. The social milieu out of which these thousands of cases arose was a continuing holocaust, the full extent and fury and meaning and end of which no one knew, but which carried dark portents. Enormous amounts of property were being destroyed through fire and looting. That all those arrested—with allowances for the inevitable few errors—were caught in a lawless activity to which they could easily and readily return when released after arraignment was apparent to all who cared to look at the situation realistically. They had already demonstrated a proclivity to lawlessness. In the event, 48.6 per cent of those persons arrested had previous criminal records, and goodly numbers of "wanted" persons were apprehended.

If each of those arrested had been released on his personal recognizance, there was danger of contempt replacing respect and sober regard for the machinery of law enforcement which might impel him to new acts of lawlessness. What service would it have been to the prisoner or the community to release one caught *flagrante delicto* looting when the Governor of the State informed the President of the United States that he was not sure that he could maintain law and order in the streets of Detroit? I had stated unequivocally on television soon after the rioting began that those responsible for lawless behavior would be prosecuted to the full extent of their criminality. Bail commensurate with the seriousness of the offense, when related to the exigencies of the sociolegal situation in the city, effectively served notice that there was meaning behind this statement.

As soon as a person was arraigned, it became the duty of the sheriff of the county to keep him in his custody until trial or until he made bail. But the county jail was close to being filled with "normal" numbers of prisoners. There was little place to put those arrested in the riot. Some were crowded in, but many had to be transferred to the jail of contiguous counties and those farther removed, and to the Federal prison at Milan, forty-five miles from Detroit, and to the state prison at Jackson, some seventy miles from Detroit, and, finally, to the bath house on Belle Isle, a public park in the middle of the Detroit River.

After bail was set by the Court, every effort was made to obtain a check on the criminal record of the defendant. This was a horrendously large job for two reasons: First, in at least half the cases two checks had to be made. If the defendant had a previous criminal record it could be found by an alphabetical check of his name in a matter of minutes, but if he had none, a fingerprint check had to be made to make sure he had not given a fictitious name. The fingerprint checks each took about one-half hour. Second, there was a shortage of experienced persons to check the files by means of fingerprints. Experts from the Police Department in Windsor, across the river in Canada, volunteered, and their help was eagerly and appreciatively accepted. The expedient of sending two men to the FBI headquarters in Washington with the prints of one thousand persons for a check of the criminal records in Washington, and then flying them back, was also helpful.

Nonetheless, the people in the Detroit record office did a trojan job. As soon as the previous arrest record of a prisoner had been obtained, the office of the Prosecuting Attorney sought to bring the prisoner back before the Court for a review of his bail. But this was not so easily done as said. When the prisoners were transferred by the sheriff to other jails in Michigan, records of these transfers were of course made, but the information from these records could not be readily ascertained. It was, therefore, a slow process to determine where a prisoner was being housed before arrangements could be made to bring him back before the Court. When the situation in the streets began returning to normal, the Court in hundreds of cases reduced bail.

Most defendants were not represented by counsel at their arraignments on the warrant. Because of the chaos in the streets, most could not be located by relatives. And then again, most could not afford an attorney. However, attorneys from the local bar association were present throughout much of the arraignments as observers. Although there were some criticisms voiced, no one at that time suggested any alternate procedures that would have been helpful.

In the circumstances that prevailed, some poignant cases of inconvenience occurred to the regret of all involved. But on the whole, those who were arrested were lawfully and properly arrested, were arraigned in court as expeditiously as circumstances allowed, were fairly bailed in face of the near anarchy which prevailed in many sections of the city, and were accorded their constitutional rights.

By statute[5] the Governor has the authority to declare that an emergency exists in a defined geographical area of the state and then subsequently by executive order to proscribe certain activities such as persons being on the streets after a certain hour, the selling of gasoline except during prescribed hours of the day, the selling of liquor, firearms, and other acts in order to mitigate the dangers of the situation. Violations of the provisions of the executive orders were declared to be misdemeanors.

There were 1,652 arrests for misdemeanors. The bulk of these were on the charge of violating curfew. These misdemeanor cases were disposed of in the courts expeditiously. Most pleaded guilty; most of the rest were found guilty. Almost all were sentenced to the time which they had spent in jail following their arrests until their release on bond, a period of five to ten days. The misdemeanor docket, it might be said, was cleaned up without any particular problems.

[5] Act 302, P.A. 1948.

In each felony case, however, the defendant had the right to demand an examination. And many hundreds of defendants did. This posed several problems. The first was to see that each defendant was represented by counsel. It would have been prohibitively costly for the courts to appoint counsel in each case at the usual rate of compensation which prevailed in our jurisdiction. Fortunately, and to the great credit of the members of the legal profession in Wayne County, large numbers of attorneys volunteered their assistance to the courts on a gratis basis. These public-spirited attorneys were assigned to represent indigent defendants. It is estimated that 30 per cent of the defendants had retained counsel.

Examination dockets were drawn for each of the 13 Recorder's Court judges. The plan devised was to interrupt the normal flow of cases through the court until all the riot cases were moved through all pre-trial stages, such as examination and arraignment on the information. Teams of defense attorneys were assigned to a particular courtroom rather than to a particular defendant. Those attorneys assigned to a particular courtroom represented all the defendants whose cases were assigned to that courtroom. While an attorney was conducting an examination, others were interviewing defendants and preparing their cases. In those instances where defense counsel needed more time to prepare, the Court granted an adjournment.

Some business firms were the complainant in a large number of cases. The A & P Company, for example, had several of its supermarkets looted. To obviate the vexatious need for such complainant to run from courtroom to courtroom looking for its cases, all cases involving the same complainant were assigned to one courtroom.

The examination dockets moved along smoothly and swiftly. All defendants were properly represented by counsel. It is significant that there has been no criticism whatever of this phase of court proceedings in connection with the riot cases. The examinations were concluded within two weeks.

For those defendants who were bound over on examination and those who waived examination, an Information had to be drafted formally stating the charge against them to which the defendant was required to plead. Here another bottleneck developed because of the sheer volume of work. It was broken by the expedient of having a special Information form printed to eliminate typing and the employment of volunteer workers from religious orders and student bodies in the court clerk's office to run down files and collate various papers and pleadings.

All defendants who were arraigned on an Information were represented by counsel because, again, public-spirited members of the local bar volunteered their services for this important function. Those arraigned on an Information are now awaiting trial.

The situation in Detroit, so far as the administration of justice was concerned during the riot was "normalcy," except that there was a lot more of it to cope with. The prisoners of the riot were processed in exactly the same manner as the arrestee in "normal" times. The only difference was "a lot more."

This "lot more" was what really gave us our difficulty. I think that if we had from the outset sufficient detention areas close to the courthouse so that the prisoners would be housed as rapidly as they were arrested and in an orderly fashion so that each could be found almost instantaneously when wanted and needed, 75 per cent of the problems which plagued us would not have. Therefore, my first advice is: arrange to have on a standby basis a sufficiently large detention area conveniently located to the courts so that those arrested can be channeled quickly and orderly from the precinct stations into this area, thus freeing up the precinct detention cells for subsequent arrestees.

The rest of the problems were simply mechanical ones of handling the enormous volume of paper work quickly and efficiently. All staffs are, of course, no larger than the normal flow of work requires; it would be wasteful of the taxpayers' money were they larger. When the volume of work handled by this staff increases prodigiously and instantly, provision must be made to augment that staff so that the increased volume of work required might be obtained.

So my second advice is: make plans to add quickly to the staff where bottlenecks are likely to develop, such as in the preparation of the complaint and warrant, the making up of files and the pulling of files. It is important not only to have personnel on a standby basis who have been initiated into the arcana of legal forms, but it is absolutely necessary that provision be made to supply them with the tools to get the job done, such as typewriters, desks, staple machines, etc. Details not readily noticed are of extreme importance. For instance, the desks provided for the additional help should be of the proper

height for typing; otherwise, the typewriters are prac-
tically useless. Also, sufficient electrical outlets for the
additional typewriters should be present. If not, typewriters will not have the current to make them go or
fuses will blow.

And since it can be anticipated that normal public
transportation will be interrupted, one person should be
charged with the task of arranging transportation for
those needed to keep the processes of justice running.
And detailed plans for the provision of food and supplies
for these people should be made because retail services
will surely be disrupted.

Other governmental offices probably will be shut during the period of disturbances but their personnel, equipment, and space should not be permitted to go unutilized.
Arrangements should be made to familiarize persons in
other divisions of government with the procedures necessary to keep the wheels of the judicial process turning so
that at a moment's notice they can pitch in to help with
the sudden increase in volume.

During extraordinary times it frequently happens that
more copies of documents are needed than normally because more agencies of government are involved. It is
important, therefore, that records be kept from the very
outset, and it is a good idea automatically to make an
extra copy of all records and documents to provide for
the unforeseen need.

It was our decision upon retrospect that it was a mis-
take to arraign the riot prisoners before a check was made
for their arrest and conviction records because this meant
that each person who was arraigned without his record

had to be brought into court a second subsequent time after his record had been checked. This taxed the police personnel whose job it was to bring the prisoners to and from the courtrooms. Just imagine how many times cell doors had to be clanged open and shut on these thousands of prisoners.

By statute in Michigan[6] a peace officer is required to take his prisoner before the most convenient magistrate without unnecessary delay. It is felt that waiting for a prisoner's record to be compiled through a search of police records is not an unnecessary delay in taking the prisoner before a magistrate.

However, for this to be done, it is necessary that additional fingerprint specialists be lined up so that they might be called into service on a moment's notice. And it should be assured that there is enough elbow room in the records room to allow additional persons to work at the records.

Lastly, but not the least in importance, the most experienced assistant prosecutors should be assigned to the task of recommending warrants. At the very beginning of the process, much unnecessary volume can be eliminated from the flow and kept out of the courts, thus easing the clerical and custodial load through the proper screening of the police write-ups and the refusal of warrants where the facts do not justify them. At times like these some are arrested who, although technically wrong for one reason or another (like being out past curfew a half hour), are

[6] "A peace officer who has arrested a person without warrant must, without unnecessary delay, take the person arrested before the most convenient magistrate of the county in which the offense was committed, and must take before the magistrate a complaint, stating the offense for which the person was arrested." C.L. '48, 764.14.

not serious law violators. These might safely be sent home with a warning while the full machinery of the law is applied to those who are bent on damaging our society permanently.

There were many persons and groups who were very much concerned during the riot with our procedures and the manner in which those who were arrested were being handled. Their concern was laudable and very much welcomed by our office. We maintained an open-door policy. All who had a legitimate interest in the procedures being followed were permitted to observe all phases of the judicial processing of prisoners, and any questions which they had were freely and openly answered. We are glad we followed this policy not only because it is unquestionably basically right but because it established confidence in all sections of the community through the allaying of fears that the law was not being impartially yet firmly administered. In the end this obviated resentment and animosity, and led to cooperation and the repair of rents in the social fabric.

About the Author

Judge James H. Lincoln was born near Harbor Beach, Michigan, majored in history at the University of Michigan, and attended Georgetown and University of Detroit Law Schools, receiving his law degree from the Detroit College of Law. He has been a law partner of Governor G. Mennen Williams, was nominated for mayor of Detroit in 1953, was twice elected to the Common Council in Detroit and twice elected Probate Judge of Wayne County, where he has served as Juvenile Court Judge since 1960.

The author, his wife, and their four children live in Detroit.

4/30/70

57254

KFM
4799
.W32
C75

Lincoln, James
        The anatomy of
a riot.

DATE DUE

APR 28 1994

GAYLORD   PRINTED IN U.S.A.